Biological and Chemical Weapons

D1372966

Other books in the At Issue series:

Alternatives to Prisons
Anorexia
Antidepressants
Anti-Semitism
Are Privacy Rights Being Violated?
Child Labor and Sweatshops
Child Sexual Abuse
Cosmetic Surgery
Creationism Versus Evolution
Do Children Have Rights?
Does Advertising Promote Substance Abuse?
Does the Internet Benefit Society?
Does the Internet Increase the Risk of Crime?
Does the United States Need a National Health Insurance
    Policy?
The Ethics of Abortion
The Future of the Internet
How Can the Poor Be Helped?
How Should One Cope with Death?
How Should Society Address the Needs of the Elderly?
How Should the United States Treat Prisoners in the War on
    Terror?
Indian Gaming
Is American Culture in Decline?
Is Islam a Religion of War or Peace?
Islam in America
Is the Gap Between Rich and Poor Growing?
Is the World Heading Toward an Energy Crisis?
Is Torture Ever Justified?
Legalizing Drugs
Managing America's Forests
Nuclear and Toxic Waste
Protecting America's Borders
Rain Forests
Religion and Education
The Right to Die
Steroids
What Causes Addiction?
What Is the State of Human Rights?

At ✳ Issue

Biological and Chemical Weapons

Stuart A. Kallen, *Book Editor*

Bruce Glassman, *Vice President*
Bonnie Szumski, *Publisher*
Helen Cothran, *Managing Editor*

GREENHAVEN PRESS
An imprint of Thomson Gale, a part of The Thomson Corporation

THOMSON
━━━━✳━━━━ ™
GALE

Detroit • New York • San Francisco • San Diego • New Haven, Conn.
Waterville, Maine • London • Munich

11. The Use of Nonlethal Chemical Weapons Should   89
    Be Prohibited
    Mark Wheelis

Organizations to Contact   99

Bibliography   103

Index   106

Introduction

On September 18, 2001, letters containing anthrax were received by the *New York Post* and the news divisions of ABC, CBS, and NBC in New York City. Around the same time, another letter containing anthrax was sent to the tabloid newspaper, the *Sun*, in Boca Raton, Florida. This last letter was opened by sixty-three-year-old picture editor Robert Stevens. On October 2, Stevens began vomiting and drifting in and out of consciousness. Three days later he was dead, killed by an anthrax infection in his lungs.

A week after Stevens died, anthrax-infected letters were received in the offices of two U.S. senators, Tom Daschle of South Dakota, and Patrick Leahy of Vermont (neither Senator came in contact with the agent). These strains of anthrax were "weapons-grade," of much higher quality and more deadly than the original material sent to New York and Florida. The death toll from the anthrax-contaminated letter attack rose to five as two mail handlers died along with two women whose mail had simply been in close contact with the letters sent to the senators. These deaths, coming so soon after the devastating September 11, 2001, terrorist attacks, left millions of Americans feeling vulnerable and afraid. A poll conducted by Reuters several weeks after the anthrax attack showed that 54 percent of Americans were concerned that they or a relative or close friend might become an anthrax victim.

Although the anthrax attacks ended as suddenly as they started, they ignited fears that terrorists might launch a large-scale bioweapons attack. United Nations secretary-general Kofi Annan expressed the anxieties of many, stating, "It is hard to imagine how the tragedy of September 11 could have been worse. Yet, the truth is that a single attack involving a . . . biological weapon could . . . [kill] millions."

Concerns were also raised that terrorists could use chemical weapons in an attack. The chemicals used in such weapons, some of which are easily produced in industrial facilities, include choking agents such as chlorine that fill the lungs with fluids, thereby asphyxiating the victim. They also include nerve agents such as VX, tabun, and sarin gases, which paralyze the central nervous system, causing victims to twitch, vomit, lose consciousness, and stop breathing. A 2001 report by the Central Intelligence Agency explained that terrorist groups are "most interested in chemicals such as cyanide salts to contaminate food and water supplies or to assassinate individuals." Such groups also have "expressed interest in many other toxic industrial chemicals . . . and traditional chemical agents, including chlorine and [the poison gas] phosgene," which are widely used in industry.

Such statements—along with the attacks themselves—quickly spread panic throughout the United States. On the Internet and at military supply stores, gas masks sold for two or three times their previous prices. Stores that sold duct tape and plastic sheeting reported brisk sales as people stocked up on items used to seal off rooms in case of attacks. In some places, doctors were inundated with requests for the antibiotic Cipro—an antidote to anthrax—although experts warned that indiscriminate use of the drug could be harmful. As journalist Stephen Stetson wrote on October 18, 2001,

> Despite Cipro's inability to act as a vaccine for anthrax, the millions trying to get prescriptions are presumably expecting to be a victim of the next anthrax-laced letter. Regardless of warnings from pharmacists that [unused] Cipro will expire and become toxic, normally mild-mannered Americans have become drug-crazed pill poppers, even getting small children on the drug, despite serious risks to their health.

The public response to the anthrax attack was covered nearly nonstop in the media. Driven by the news, jittery citizens began calling authorities when unidentified bags of white powder were found. In Florida alone police received more than one hundred calls about suspicious powders that all turned out to be innocuous substances such as sugar and plaster dust. In Trenton, New Jersey, two office buildings were evacuated after employees reported opening packages containing powder. Tests found no traces of any pathogens in the containers.

Meanwhile, the Federal Bureau of Investigation searched in vain to find the person or persons who had launched the anthrax attacks. Although the anthrax strain in all the letters was from a type commonly found in U.S. research labs, responsibility was variously assigned to Iraqi, Afghani, or Iranian terrorists, or unemployed scientists from the former Soviet Union. The culprit was never identified.

The anthrax attacks made millions of people keenly aware of the perils of biological and chemical weapons. Many were alarmed to discover that someone armed with a basic knowledge of science—and instructions available on the Internet—might be able to construct a bioweapon. President George W. Bush reinforced the fears of many, stating,

> Armed with a single vial of a biological agent . . . small groups of fanatics, or failing states, could gain the power to threaten great nations, threaten the world peace. America, and the entire civilized world, will face this threat for decades to come. We must confront the danger with open eyes, and unbending purpose.

Such frightening scenarios prompted the U.S. government to institute measures to counter the spread of biological and chemical weapons. In 2001 Congress budgeted more than $2.5 billion for programs to defend the country from biological and chemical attacks. By 2005 that amount jumped to $7.6 billion.

Despite this investment, many experts believe that some hostile group or individual will eventually try to launch a biological or chemical attack against Americans. High-tech defense measures—or simple good police work—may suffice to protect U.S. civilians and military personnel. Whether the necessary protections will be in place if needed is as much an issue as whether they will be effective. What is certain is that a single terrorist with a small amount of a deadly substance can quickly spread panic throughout society. While the number of casualties from such an attack might be low, the far-reaching consequence would be a society riddled with fear of being attacked by an unseen enemy.

sponse efforts. Yet, the human impact and economic impact of 11 September 2001 will be dwarfed if adversaries are able to effectively deploy mass-casualty biological weapons against the United States. Unless we focus appropriate dollars and develop a coherent national plan to prepare for and prevent such actions, the United States will likely suffer an enormous economic loss that could even lead to our demise as a superpower.

Will There Be an Attack?

A belief in one or more of at least six false assumptions or myths helps explain why individuals, including senior civilian and military leaders, do not believe that a mass-casualty BW attack will occur.

Myth One: There Has Never Been a Significant BW Attack

This contention is counter to historical fact. Even before the fall 2001 anthrax terrorism in the United States, incidents of BW and bio-terrorism have occurred on multiple occasions. Today, more countries have active BW programs than at any other time in history, which increases the likelihood that BW will be used again in the future.

Military organizations have used biological weapons many times. . . . The Germans used anthrax (*Bacillus anthracis*) and glanders (*Pseudomonas mallei*) against the horses and mules of the US Army and its Allies in World War I. . . . The *Textbook for Military Medicine*, published in 1997, states that an estimated 10,923 deaths resulted from the Soviet use of chemical and biological warfare (CBW) agents in Afghanistan, Laos, and Kampuchea (Cambodia). In 2001, the US Senate and other US government offices were attacked through the mail system by letters filled with lethal anthrax spores milled to the 1–5 micron size, which can inflict death from inhalation. BW, it must be concluded, has been an accepted practice for a number of states for a long time.

Myth Two: The United States Has Never Been Attacked by a BW Agent

Counting the 2001 anthrax attacks, there are at least six known instances where BW has been used against US citizens or resources. The British were alleged to have used smallpox in the Revolutionary War. The Germans used glanders . . . during World War I. The Japanese used multiple biological agents against their foes during World War II. The Aum Shinrikyo cult failed in 1990 in its botulinum toxin attack on the two US naval bases located at Yokosuka and Yokohama. In 1984, the Bhagwan Shree Rajneesh cult contaminated 10 restaurant salad bars in Oregon with salmonella and infected at least 750 local citizens. This BW attack, like the naval base attacks, was not discovered until several years after the event. Proliferation experts, such as the National Defense University's Seth Carus, agree that these examples lend credence to the possibility that the United States may have unknowingly fallen victim to still other BW attacks in the past.

Myth Three: You Have to Be Extremely Intelligent, Highly Educated, and Well Funded

Financial status or brilliance is no longer a major roadblock for an individual or group to acquire a significant BW capability. Dr. Tara O'Toole, deputy director for the Center for Civilian Biodefense Studies at Johns Hopkins University, believes we have probably crossed over the threshold from "too difficult" to accomplish to "doable by a determined individual or group." It is true that there are certain technical hurdles, but there are many thousands of highly educated microbiologists or other health science professionals worldwide that are capable of growing, weaponizing, and employing a BW agent. Much of the technical information is readily available on the Internet, in libraries, and through mail-order channels that provide "how-to" manuals. For example, Steve Priesler, who has a degree in chemistry, wrote such a manual and made it available on the Internet for only $18. This manual, titled *Silent Death* by "Uncle Fester," tells the reader where to find, grow, and weaponize agents such as *Bacillus anthracis* and *Clostridium botulinum;* it also instructs the reader on how to employ the agents to kill small or large numbers of people.

Myth Four: Biological Warfare Must Be Too Difficult Because It Has Failed

Most of the BW attempts mentioned in this article resulted in deaths or casualties. However, not all attempts in the past have been successful. For example, it was not known until 1995 attack is made on an adversary's military installation. That attack could render the installation nonfunctional within 72 hours. The first clinical cases of anthrax would probably manifest themselves in around 24 hours, with the number of subsequent cases increasing rapidly. A follow-on conventional military attack that was timed to occur three to four days after the BW attack would likely find the installation defenders laid low by the disease and therefore would be more likely to succeed. Moreover, because of the nature of the *Bacillus anthracis* organism, the attackers would not have to be overly concerned about significant secondary infections from their infected adversaries or by large amounts of residual spores in the environment.

> *We can look to the emergence of organizations such as al Qaida . . . and see that any previous moral constraints to inflicting massive civilian deaths are no longer applicable.*

The second scenario involves an attack on an adversary's population or military installation with Q fever ([caused by the bacterium] *Coxiella burnetii*). With Q fever's two- to 10-day incubation period, the attacker and his followers would have days to escape before their adversary would recognize that there had been an attack. Between the fifth and 10th day after the attack, the attackers could announce that a nonlethal weapon had been used as a "show of force and resolve" and demand whatever concessions they were after. The attackers would have little concern of being exposed to secondary infection because Q fever is not communicable. Likewise, the low fatality rate would take away the adversary's justification for a massive retaliation but at the same time leave the adversary's population with a heightened sense of fear because of their proven vulnerability.

What Would Motivate a BW Attack on the United States?

There are two primary motivations that might drive an adversary to attack the United States with a BW agent. Either one is enough to cause a nation, organization, or individual to act against the United States, but concerns should be particularly heightened when both of these motivations intersect.

The first motivation is to gradually "erode US influence" as a world superpower. Adversaries such as Iraq, Iran, or the al Qaida organization desire more influence in their region. They are infuriated that American infidels have increased their presence in the Middle East from three ships in 1949 to over 200,000 US military personnel in 2001. . . .

The second motivation is categorized as "revenge or hate." At a time when the United States is an integral part of stimulating the global economy and thereby improving the standard of living for millions in the world, the so-called transparency of the United States inflames envy, which often leads to hatred, in millions around the world. The United States has 5 percent of the world's population yet uses 24 percent of the global energy. The extravagance of the United States is seen by some as the reason for a worldwide moral decay. Often these same individuals may want to inflict revenge because of what they perceive the United States or its "puppet nations" have done to them individually, their family, or their group. Many of these individuals have been taught from childhood to hate the United States. This prejudice often grows as they see images on television that portray the United States as a drunken, immoral, gluttonous, and violent society. . . .

Possible Future BW Scenarios

This author believes that there are three most likely BW scenarios the United States and its allies might face in the future:
- An agroterrorist event against the United States,
- A BW attack on United States and allied troops in the Middle East, and/or
- A bioterrorist attack against a large population center in the United States or an allied state.

Scenario One: An Agroterrorist Event

[Science and technology expert] Anne Kohnen states that "agricultural targets are soft targets," or ones that maintain such a low level of security that a terrorist could carry out an attack unobserved. Biological agents are small, inexpensive, and nearly impossible to detect. A terrorist may choose to use BW against agriculture simply because it is the easiest and cheapest way to cause large-scale damage.". . .

Such an incident in the United States could potentially jeopardize $140 billion in yearly pork, beef, and poultry exports. . . .

This type of attack has an added benefit for the adversary: unless he desires otherwise, he may never be identified. Since the goal is not to achieve attention, but to promote the demise of and inflict pain on the United States, the perpetrators could maintain a safe distance and enjoy the daily news of turmoil in the United States. They could watch the successful completion of their plan as the contagious nature of their weapon operated on its own—the gift that keeps on giving. Perpetrators willing to use this style of BW attack would have to recognize that it might take years to achieve their objective. Some world terrorists may be willing to wait and see their strategic plans carried out over this longer period of time.

Scenario Two: A BW Attack on Forces in the Middle East

This attack's goal is to have the United States withdraw its military forces from the region and possibly reduce its aid to allies like Israel. The Middle East contains more states with biological weapons than any other region of the world. According to the Center for Nonproliferation Studies at the Monterey Institute of International Studies, there are 11 states with suspected or confirmed offensive biological programs. Of these, six reside in the Middle East. Additionally, more weapons of mass destruction (WMD) attacks have occurred in the Middle East than in any other region. . . . This region of the world has an entirely different view about the use of weapons considered taboo by much of the rest of the world. . . .

> *Biological agents are small, inexpensive, and nearly impossible to detect.*

So how would a BW attack be carried out in the Middle East? There are multiple options an adversary might choose to pressure the United States to withdraw from the region. The three options discussed below are illustrative of the variety of problems those attacks could create.

An adversary might choose to use a nonlethal BW agent,

perhaps VEE (Venezuelan equine encephalitis), on a US installation. Such an attack would make personnel sick and incapacitated, but would not kill them. It could be used to demonstrate an adversary's capability, resolve, and even compassion. The adversary could allow time to ensure that the attack was effective, that deaths were minimal, that people were recovering, and then announce why and what he had done. If the BW attack failed, then the adversary would not make an announcement or lose credibility. Likewise, if the attack caused many unexpected deaths, he could merely remain quiet and potentially avoid US retaliation. . . .

This approach would likely trigger great debates in Washington, D.C., and Middle Eastern countries, and might even cause the US Congress to pressure the president to withdraw US forces. If the United States then elected to stay in the region and a lethal attack did occur, local populations around US bases would die along with the targeted Americans. Thereafter, local governments would be under enormous pressure and might choose to ask the United States to withdraw rather than suffer additional BW attacks on their populations.

> *Hundreds of thousands of American citizens could potentially become infected and die if the agent were correctly manufactured and employed.*

Another option an adversary might choose would be to release a lethal agent just outside a US base so that the wind would carry it away from the base. A desirable effect could be achieved by even a small attack aimed at killing as few as 20 to 50 of the local population. The downwind casualties would be blamed on the Americans, creating a local mistrust of the American government. The responsible group would never claim credit but would inform, the media and others that the deaths were caused by US BW agents (even though the United States does not have any offensive BW agents). It's likely that the regional media would have a "heyday," which would lead to a groundswell of anger against the United States. . . . A continued US presence in the region could become politically impossible to maintain. Such small-scale attacks could be repeated over and over with lethal or nonlethal BW agents.

An adversary could also use a lethal agent directly against a US installation in the region. The adversary would never claim credit for this attack option, but might release a small dose of BW agent like anthrax or tularemia to try to kill two to 10 Americans. These deaths could raise fear of future lethal attacks and cause US officials and members of Congress to debate the merit of a continued US presence in the Middle East. . . .

Scenario Three: A Bioterrorist Attack on a Large US Center

Similar to the 11 September attacks, a BW attack might be a co-ordinated attack and take place in several major US cities. Anthrax would probably be the agent of choice in a mass-casualty attempt since it is not contagious and the perpetrators would not have to worry about the disease getting back to their country. Five 100-pound bags of anthrax could easily be smuggled into the United States using one of the many shipments of grain that arrive at US ports every day. These bags could be made to blend in with the shipment and lined with plastic so that no powder would be prematurely released. Three to five major cities, on the order of Houston or Los Angeles, could be targeted and would require only a 100-pound bag each. An appropriate aerosolizing device, easily procured in the United States, could be mounted on an automobile, airplane, or boat. The terrorists that perpetrate this attack would not have to die because they could be vaccinated and treated with antibiotics prior to delivering the agents, which would protect them even if they were exposed. They could also easily depart the country before the first symptoms appeared and defeat the ability of federal authorities to respond and arrest them.

Hundreds of thousands of American citizens could potentially become infected and die if the agent were correctly manufactured and employed and if optimal climatic conditions were present during the attack. Such a mass-casualty attack would overwhelm the US medical system and a human, economic, and political catastrophe would result.

Billions of Dollars Are Needed

Many of our national leaders still do not believe that a mass-casualty BW event will happen in the next 10 years—in spite of our experience with the anthrax attacks that followed the 11 September 2001 attacks. This view is based on their belief in one of the several myths discussed in this article. Such myths continue to inhibit the adequate funding of US and allied bio-defense.

US national security leaders must appreciate the urgency to refocus programs and develop appropriate budgets to support a concerted biodefense effort to counter BW possibilities. The counteragroterrorism effort is woefully underfunded. This program is of extreme importance, and it needs billions of additional dollars to upgrade the protection of our agricultural industry. . . .

One of the most horrifying possibilities would be a coordinated and simultaneous BW attack against several major cities in the United States and in allied countries. Those attacks could occur today, and we might not become aware of them for days. A series of major exercises have documented the likely and frightening results; many hundreds of thousands could die, and US and allied societies could be thrown into chaos and panic.

Myths to the contrary, the biological warfare and bioterrorist threats are real and require the full commitment of the United States and its allies to have a well-funded biodefense effort to produce an effective defense. The United States must take up the yoke of preventing such attacks and prepare for consequence management—managing the aftermath of such attacks—with the same vigor our nation used during the cold war. Otherwise, our national security stands in jeopardy.

actual risk to individual citizens remains quite low. Americans may be harboring any number of nightmare scenarios involving biological or chemical weapons. But there are good reasons why we shouldn't be worrying too much about these threats.

Anthrax, for instance, is not contagious, and technology is being developed to neutralize its spores. A small deployment of anthrax is the most we should fear—and as they were in fall of 2001, containment and decontamination should be effective tactics in limiting the loss of life from any such attack. The hoarding of perishable antibiotics without a prescription is not only fruitless, it is also expensive. Doctors ought to be discouraging this habit; ditto for the anthrax vaccine, which can cause flu-like symptoms and does not prevent anthrax, but only lessens its severity.

> *Duct tape and plastic sheets? To protect us from what? How is a terrorist going to bring VX gas to my door?*

Smallpox is another risk that keeps some Americans awake at night. But because the disease is only communicable from person to person, it can be contained by quarantining victims and vaccinating others after it appears. Even among those unfortunate few who would be infected, the death toll would still be less than 10 percent. And even weaponized smallpox could be kept contained. As far as smallpox vaccinations [go], though the live-virus vaccine has well documented side effects—including the spread of a related virus, brain swelling and skin conditions—there is no need to fear it. If necessary, this vaccine and others would prove relatively safe for use on a wide scale. Right now, however, it is not necessary to vaccinate anyone besides first responders.

The bubonic plague requires fleas to be spread, and public-health measures would be able to limit the disease's reach relatively easily should it be used in a terrorist attack. The last time the bubonic plague was deployed as a weapon—in China during World War II—the Chinese public-health system did not contain it particularly effectively. Today, the American public-health system would.

The threat we face from chemical terrorist attacks has been

similarly exaggerated. Nerve gas is very difficult to produce and to distribute; moreover, it dissipates rapidly. As for sarin gas, when it was released in the Tokyo subway system in 1995, a lot more fear than gas ended up being spread. (Only a dozen people actually died in Japan during that attack.) VX gas is more deadly because it stays around longer and can stick to your skin, enter your pores and block all your nerves—but it would be just about impossible for clouds of VX gas to blow through the streets. A delivery system that could expose a massive number of citizens to nerve gas without the gas being destroyed by heat or dissipated by wind simply doesn't exist. Duct tape and plastic sheets? To protect us from what? How is a terrorist going to bring VX gas to my door?

Personalizing Threats

We need to see such risks in just these kinds of terms in order to combat them psychologically. We need to understand that our fear causes us to mythologize these weapons, which have already taken on enlarged significance in our collective imagination because some have been used in the past for evil purposes. But fear of these diseases and chemicals far outweighs their actual risk to us. Here in the United States, an unsexy virus not much associated with evil or terrorism—influenza—claims between 10,000 and 20,000 lives per year; smallpox hasn't taken a life since the 1970s.

> *An unsexy virus not much associated with evil or terrorism—influenza—claims between 10,000 and 20,000 lives per year; smallpox hasn't taken a life since the 1970s.*

So why are alerts taken so seriously if the potential for terrorists to use biological or chemical weapons on a large scale is so small? First of all, we are [fighting] a war. . . . People may be personalizing and localizing their general sense of the vulnerability of U.S. soldiers and U.S. interests. Many have wondered whether a war in the Persian Gulf could trigger the use of weapons of mass destruction on our soil, either by a proxy for the Iraqi regime or al-Qaeda terrorists. Unfortunately the "preparations" for such an attack—unlikely though it may be—create a great deal of anxiety. And the cold truth is that holding a gas mask or a roll of duct tape or a box of Cipro in your hands should not provide reassurance to a rational person. "When do I use this tape or this gas mask?" my patients ask me. The answer is that in the one-in-a-billion chance they would ever need it, they probably wouldn't have the time or know-how to employ it.

In any event, it would be difficult to deploy weapons of mass destruction on a broad scale within our borders. As a result, in all likelihood, the most we have to fear on this side of the ocean are conventional terrorist attacks. But meanwhile we are left to imagine—erroneously—something far worse.

Our elected officials understandably don't want to be criticized for not having warned us should an unconventional terrorist attack take place. Only five people died from anthrax exposure during the scare following September 11. Yet many subsequently criticized the FBI, the Centers for Disease Control and Prevention, and other agencies for a lack of preparation and cooperation. So this time around, President Bush and his administration have opted to panic the country in advance. But they would do well to remember that for 50 years Americans lived with daily threats far scarier—if perhaps more predictable—than those we face today. As I remind my patients, we got used to them then. And we will now.

3

Sabotage at Chemical Factories Presents a Greater Risk than Do Chemical Weapons

Sabrina McLaughlin

Sabrina McLaughlin is a journalist whose articles appear in Current Science.

The deadly effects of chemical weapons such as mustard gas and nerve gas are well known. In 1988 Iraqi leader Saddam Hussein used these chemicals against Kurds in Iraq, killing more than five thousand. While the public is understandably frightened of chemical weapons in the hands of terrorists, it is doubtful that such devices could ever be utilized to launch a large-scale attack in the United States. Use of chemical weapons requires technical skills and sophisticated delivery systems that are unavailable to terrorists. Of greater threat to the safety and security of Americans are industrial chemical plants that are located in every state, often near major population centers. Determined terrorists could sabotage a plant that manufactures chemicals, causing harm to many and threatening millions. While the government is calling on the chemical industry to improve security measures, factory owners are required only to submit worst-case scenarios to the U.S. Environmental Protection Agency; nothing compels them to improve security or to change their practices. Until strict security measures are mandated for the chemical industry, mil-

lions of Americans are at risk from deadly chemicals produced in their cities and towns.

In March 1988, the Iraqi government launched an assault on
Halabja, a town in Iraq populated by Kurdish people. For
three nights, Iraqi airplanes bombarded the town, killing more
than 5,000 Kurds. The Iraqi forces unleashed on Halabja a
"cocktail" of at least four chemical weapons—mustard gas [and
three other poison gases], sarin, tabun, and VX. A chemical
weapon is a poisonous substance that injures or kills people.

> *A determined terrorist might rain down chemical weapons from a low-flying plane, rig them on bombs or spray them from the ground.*

Chemical weapons are one part of the package widely
known as weapons of mass destruction (WMDs)—weapons
that have the potential to inflict immediate, widespread harm.
WMDs also include biological and nuclear weapons.

Prior to the U.S.-led invasion of Iraq [in] March [2003], the
Bush administration repeatedly warned that the Iraqi government possessed WMDs that threatened the United States and
other countries. "The security of the world requires disarming
Hussein," said Bush. . . . No chemical or other WMDs [were ever]
found in Iraq.

Under what conditions could chemical weapons, used by
any enemy, cause harm?

Death by Chemistry

Chemical weapons are the cheapest and easiest WMDs to ob-
tain. They can be made in the same factories that manufacture
chemicals for industrial or agricultural use.

Chemical weapons are stored in an easy-to-handle liquid
form and are dispersed into the air as vapors or aerosols. A va-
por is a type of gas, and an aerosol is a suspension of tiny liquid or solid particles in a gas. A determined terrorist might rain
down chemical weapons from a low-flying plane, rig them on
bombs or spray them from the ground.

As frightening as that might sound, chemical weapons are usually ineffective WMDs, says Angelo Acquista, a former director of the New York City Office of Emergency Management. "We all have this image of a crop plane spraying a crowd with some chemical agent, and that's not likely to happen . . . because of the environmental limitations," Acquista told the Cincinnati Enquirer.

A successful chemical attack requires specific conditions: indirect sunlight, warm temperatures, steady breezes, and the absence of precipitation. Without those conditions, the chemicals weaken.

A 1993 study by the U.S. Office of Technology Assessment estimated that attackers could kill 8,000 Americans by releasing a ton of the chemical weapon sarin on an "ideal" day. However, a slight shift in the weather would lower that death toll by 90 percent.

Sarin degrades quickly in cool temperatures, according to the Chemical and Biological Arms Control Institute. It also hydrolyzes in rain or humid air. Hydrolysis is the splitting of a chemical compound into two or more new substances as it reacts to water.

> *Mass destruction is much easier to achieve with conventional weapons, such as artillery shells, bombs, and bullets.*

In 1995, a Japanese cult released sarin in the Tokyo subway during rush hour. Twelve people died and thousands were hurt. The attack succeeded because the nerve agent was released in an enclosed, poorly ventilated area. The Iraqi military also gassed the Kurds of Halabja under ideal conditions. The military had time to test wind speed and direction. It also commanded dozens of fighter-bombers that attacked the defenseless Kurds over and over each night.

Chemical weapons are failure-prone in other ways. A terrorist could place them inside artillery shells, fire them at a target, and still not succeed. The impact of the shells could destroy the chemicals, says Anthony Cordesman of the Center for Strategic & International Studies. When terrorists first attacked the World Trade Center in 1993, they used explosives and deadly cyanide gas. The heat from the explosion destroyed the cyanide.

According to Amy Smithson, director of the Chemical and Biological Weapons Nonproliferation Project, mass destruction is much easier to achieve with conventional weapons, such as artillery shells, bombs, and bullets, "Yes, Al Qaeda has shown an interest in chemical . . . devices," Smithson told *USA Today*. "But in the case of terrorist activities, the statistics are stark: It's bombs, bombs, bombs."

Cause for Concern?

The most dangerous chemical threat to the United States could be sitting right in our backyards. The national chemical industry is a $450-billion business, and chemical plants exist near many major cities. If a terrorist were to crash a plane into a chemical storage tank and unleash its contents, many people could be at risk, says Smithson.

The U.S. Environmental Protection Agency (EPA) requires some chemical plants to describe what might happen to nearby populations if the contents of storage tanks were released. The EPA established the rule after a leak at a Union Carbide chemical plant in Bhopal, India, killed more than 2,000 people in 1984. The EPA says 123 chemical plants in the United States have stockpiles that each could threaten more than 1 million Americans. Another 750 plants have stockpiles that each could threaten 100,000 people.

The EPA's estimates apply only to accidents. No federal laws currently require chemical plants to assess their vulnerability to terrorist attack or to take steps to protect themselves. Some chemical companies have acted on their own to improve security. Others have not.

Will that situation change? [In 2003], a U.S. government report acknowledged that domestic chemical facilities might be at risk of terrorist attacks. The report called on government agencies, including the Office of Homeland Security, to develop an overall strategy for security at chemical plants.

4

The Chemical Industry Has Taken Steps to Prevent Terrorist Sabotage

Robert Winder

Robert Winder is the features editor for Chemistry & Industry *magazine, published by the British Society of Chemical Industry, a trade group.*

Since the terrorist attacks of September 11, 2001, the chemical industry has been on high alert. Fear of sabotage has prompted hundreds of chemical manufacturers to institute rigorous security measures. Qualified personnel have conducted risk analyses to measure plants' vulnerability, and company executives have discussed safety measures with members of the Department of Homeland Security, the FBI, and other federal agencies. In addition, more than 150 chemical plants have signed on to the Responsible Care Security Code, a program that guides factory owners in enhancing security against terrorist attacks. The chemical industry understands that it has a clear responsibility to prevent terrorism and is taking steps to ensure that all Americans will remain safe in their communities.

As a result of the terrorist attacks on New York's World Trade Center and the Pentagon in Washington, DC, on 11 September 2001, security analysts have considered chemical plants

Robert Winder, "Plant Protection," *Chemistry & Industry*, February 2, 2004. Copyright © 2004 by the Society of Chemical Industry. Reproduced by permission.

to be potential terrorist targets. Indeed, two weeks after 11 September, one German newspaper suggested [chemical manufacturer] BASF's Ludwigshafen site was the number one such target in Germany.

Fortunately, to date there have been no terror incidents at chemical plants, and there is little to suggest that chemical plants have been targeted for attack. However, journalists and representatives of environmental groups have gained access to chemical plants to highlight security holes.

Following 11 September the chemical industry, both in Europe and the US reacted quickly to develop stronger security guidelines for plants.

Late last year [2003] the American Chemistry Council (ACC) reported that each of its 154 members was implementing an extensive security programme under the chemical industry's Responsible Care Security Code. The code addresses site, transportation and cyber security. By October 2003, vulnerability assessments at the highest priority sites had been completed and the remaining assessments were due to be completed by the end of December. In January [2004], the Synthetic Organic Chemical Manufacturers Association (SOCMA) announced its members had completed security vulnerability assessments (SVAs) at their facilities. The chemical industry programme, which the ACC describes as the most aggressive in US industry, [was] commended by [former] homeland security secretary Tom Ridge, the Federal Bureau of Investigation and the General Accounting Office. The ACC [urged] the US Congress and the Administration to pass chemical industry security legislation.

> *Fortunately, to date there have been no terror incidents at chemical plants, and there is little to suggest that chemical plants have been targeted for attack.*

The ACC's Security Code required companies to rank each facility into four tiers, based on the nature of the assets at the facility, the consequences of a terrorist attack and other factors. ACC companies are using nationally recognised methods to measure how vulnerable the sites are, such as those I developed by Sandia National Laboratories [in the United States] and the

Center for Chemical Process Safety [of the American Institute of Chemical Engineers].

"Our member companies are devoting extraordinary resources and energy to securing chemical facilities against terrorist attack," says ACC president and CEO Greg Lebedev. "We were well prepared before [11 September] and we have become better prepared since.". . .

Boosting Security Measures

[The] Chemical Facilities Security Act of 2003 . . . compels chemical operators to make vulnerability assessments and site security plans, and grants authority to the US Department of Homeland Security (DHS) to regulate those plans and oversee security at the nation's chemical plants.

The legislation includes a requirement that chemical operators consider using alternative approaches in their processes, and that they submit their vulnerability assessments and security plans to the DHS. It also gives the DHS the ability to order facilities to take specific actions when faced with imminent terrorist threats.

> *The Responsible Care Security Code is designed to help protect people, property, products, processes, information and information systems by enhancing security.*

The Responsible Care Security Code is designed to help protect people, property, products, processes, information and information systems by enhancing security. This includes security against potential terrorist attack throughout the chemical industry value chain, including the design, procurement, manufacturing, marketing, distribution, transportation, customer support, use, recycling and disposal of products. The Security Code is designed to help companies achieve continuous improvement in security performance. By using a risk-based approach companies can identify, assess and address vulnerabilities, prevent or mitigate incidents, enhance training and response capabilities, and maintain and improve relationships with key stakeholders.

For the Security Code to work, companies must understand

that security is a shared responsibility requiring actions by their customers, suppliers, service providers, and government officials and agencies.

The Security Code lays down a series of practices for companies to adhere to. Senior management is expected to commit to continuous security improvement through published policies, provision of sufficient and qualified resources and established accountability. Companies need to prioritise and periodically analyse potential security threats, vulnerabilities and consequences using accepted methods. Companies should develop and implement security measures that are commensurate with risks, and should take into account inherently safer approaches to process design, engineering and administrative controls, and prevention and mitigation measures. Other measures required take into account cyber-security, correct documentation of security programmes, providing training for all employees, communication of security issues with stakeholders, and auditing security programmes to ensure they are most effective.

5

In the Germ Labs: The Former Soviet Union Had Huge Stocks of Biological Agents

Fred Guterl and Eve Conant

Fred Guterl and Eve Conant are staff writers for Newsweek.

Scientists in the former Soviet Union produced and maintained supplies of pathogens capable of transmitting anthrax, plague, and a wide array of other deadly diseases. When the country collapsed in 1992, the scientists were suddenly unemployed, and the stockpiles of these biological weapons materials were left largely unguarded. In the following years terrorist leader Osama bin Laden and other terrorists tried to entice unemployed scientists into producing bioweapons for use in terrorist attacks. Meanwhile, research facilities are poorly maintained, their dangerous germs vulnerable to theft. The U.S. Department of Defense has spent tens of millions of dollars to secure former bioweapons facilities, but far more is needed to do the job properly. Until these weapons labs are secured or dismantled—and bioweapons experts are employed at nonterrorist enterprises—the security of the United States is at risk.

Bakyt Atshabar has worked for the anti-plague institute for more than 25 years, and for much of that time there was little need for security guards and fences and heavy metal doors

35

with keypad locks. As an unofficial part of the Soviet Union's vast bioweapons program, the institute routinely kept dozens of different strains of anthrax, plague and tularemia stored in unlocked refrigerators. But Moscow's ironclad control over life in Kazakhstan protected the labs. So did a veil of secrecy that hid the institute's bioweapons role from local residents.

> At the Alma-Ata institute, vials of anthrax are kept in coffee cans, which themselves are stored in a 40-year-old refrigerator secured with a simple padlock.

When the Soviet Union collapsed, however, the thick shrubs surrounding the institute's campus began to attract petty thieves and drunks. "We had bums right outside my window here," says Atshabar, now director of the institute, which is located in a leafy suburb of Alma-Ata, the largest city in Kazakhstan. "They would sleep there"—he points to a tuft of trees—"and drink vodka." Criminals once broke in and stole an aluminum part of a centrifuge, useless except as scrap metal. It would have been even easier to rob—or smuggle out—a small vial of nasty germs to sell on the black market. As far as anybody knows, no such theft ever occurred at the institute (formally known as the Kazakh Science Center for Quarantine and Zoonotic Diseases)[1] But keeping close track of pathogen cultures is next to impossible, even for the most tightly run lab. And at the Alma-Ata institute, vials of anthrax are kept in coffee cans, which themselves are stored in a 40-year-old refrigerator secured with a simple padlock.

In the wake of [the terrorist attacks on] September 11 [2001], the Big Fear—the one driving President George W. Bush's most important decisions and dire pronouncements—is that a terrorist group like Al Qaeda will eventually get its hands on weapons of mass destruction [WMD]. These worries are heightened because U.S. officials have learned that Osama bin Laden's network was trying to acquire such weapons. Documents recovered from Qaeda safe houses and camps in Afghan-

---

1. Zoonotic diseases are those that can be transmitted from animals to humans.

istan "show that bin Laden was pursuing a sophisticated biological weapons research program," CIA Director George Tenet told Congress [in early February 2002]. Bush has used such concerns to justify his warnings against Iraq, Iran and North Korea—what he calls the "axis of evil." Such countries "could provide these arms to terrorists," he declared in his State of the Union Message. In large part, it's the fear of WMD in the hands of terrorists that is behind large increases in spending on the military, and on home-land defense.

But the "rogue states" are not the only concern when it comes to WMD proliferation. Some experts worry that the countries of the former Soviet Union, with enormous stockpiles of pathogens, high levels of corruption and grim conditions for scientists, could be vulnerable to terrorists looking for highly destructive agents. Al Qaeda itself appears to have targeted ex-Soviet weapons scientists for recruitment. According to U.S. intelligence reports, some Russian experts traveled to Kandahar [Afghanistan] for job interviews with unidentified Qaeda leaders. Intelligence officials believe the Russians turned down the chance to work for bin Laden, however, and by all by accounts Al Qaeda's efforts to make or acquire bioweapons have gone nowhere.

> *At their peak, the Soviets probably employed upwards of 60,000 people on bioweapons projects, which produced a greater volume and variety of deadly agents than any other country.*

So how worried should we be? At their peak, the Soviets probably employed upwards of 60,000 people on bioweapons projects, which produced a greater volume and variety of deadly agents than any other country. When Ken Alibek, a senior Soviet bioweapons official, defected in 1992, he described a staggering offensive bioweapons production capacity—4,500 metric tons of anthrax a year, for instance—and an alarming array of deadly pathogens, including smallpox and antibiotic-resistant anthrax.

Gennady Lepyoshkin was Alibek's deputy in the Soviet era, and later took his job as head of the giant production facility at Stepnogorsk in Kazakhstan. In its heyday, the facility, with fermenting tanks as tall as four-story buildings, could produce 1.5 tons of weaponized anthrax in only 24 hours. Lepyoshkin has more than 20 years' experience in biowarfare, a doctorate in biology and another in microbiology. Now he's unemployed. (Russian born, he was replaced recently by a Kazakh.) As he walks along the perimeter fence at Stepnogorsk, where he no longer has clearance, he drinks a shot of cognac in honor of his old haunt. "Most of our scientists left for Russia, Ukraine or Belarus," he says. "But the ones who stayed—biological and chemical engineers—make ends meet by driving to Omsk to buy sausage and cheeses and then selling them here."

Retraining Scientists

A few years ago the U.S. government estimated that 7,000 former Soviet bio-weaponeers were a "proliferation concern," says Amy Smithson, a bioweapons expert at the Stimson Center in Washington. After September 11, they upped the figure to 10,000. Suddenly, formerly benign activities began to look worrisome—veterinary institutes, for instance, hold livestock pathogens that in the wrong hands could devastate a nation's farms.

[Since 1994] the State Department has been retraining former weapons scientists and helping institutes turn their bioweapons programs into peaceful, commercial ventures. The . . . Bush administration initially regarded this—and similar efforts to help Russian scientists—with deep suspicion. But 9-11 changed that. Now the Defense Department's work on former Soviet bioweapons facilities is to be greatly expanded, from $17 million in the current fiscal year to $55 million. Early [in 2002] the State Department's assistance program received a one-time appropriation of $30 million . . . to dismantle the Stepnogorsk military fermenters and put former Soviet scientists to work making vaccines. "They do a great job with the resources they have," says Smithson, "but even with the extra money they're only getting at the tip of the iceberg."

Not everyone agrees. It would be irresponsible for an expert like Smithson not to be concerned, but many respected specialists believe the numbers of unemployed bioweapons scientists are exaggerated. Alibek, the Soviet defector, has said that there are perhaps 100 former Soviet scientists capable of building a soup-to-nuts bioweapons factory. Western bioweapons experts put that figure higher—"the low hundreds," says one. But the more important point, says an intelligence source, is that "we think we know where almost all of those people are." An effort by Iran to recruit former Soviet scientists in 1997, in fact, helped invigorate the U.S. push to pay the scientists to stay in place. "We said, 'Work with us and you will get funding for real collaborative research; work with Iran and you will never see a penny of our money'," says Elisa Harris, who handed nonproliferation programs in the Clinton administration. Experts also stress, moreover, how difficult it is to turn a pathogen into a bioweapons agent like the "aerosolized" anthrax sent through the U.S. mail system in October [2001]. (Although investigators haven't ruled out a foreign source, the prevailing theory is still that the anthrax came from within the United States.)

But what about ready-made stockpiles of weaponized agents, or even just virulent strains? Two years ago the [Defense Department] began helping former Soviet bioweapons labs to beef up security. The institute in Alma-Ata, which houses cultures of nonweaponized, but still dangerous, germs, now boasts a 2.5-meter concrete wall topped with barbed wire. Two guards armed with stun guns and tear gas patrol the front and rear entrances. But still, nobody is searched upon entering or leaving the building. And on a recent visit, no security guards were posted at the door to the "highly hazardous infections" wing.

The larger problem is that the Alma-Ata lab is about as good as it gets. Kazakhstan alone has eight other anti-plague institutes and about 140 minor labs. None of them have had the benefit of the [U.S. Defense Department] program. Beyond Kazakhstan, throughout the ruins of the Soviet empire, hundreds of laboratories holding samples of bioweapons agents also are poorly guarded. September 11 spurred the Bush administration to take the issue more seriously. But when success includes anthrax vials in coffee cans, it'll be a long time, if ever, before anybody feels absolutely secure.

6

Government Bioweapons Research Labs Could Threaten Nearby Communities

Dee Ann Divis and Nicholas M. Horrock

Dee Ann Divis, the senior science and technology editor for United Press International (UPI), focuses on bioterrorism and the connection between government policy and technology. Nicholas M. Horrock is UPI's chief White House correspondent.

In an effort to step up research on bioweapons, the federal government conducts research at about twenty centers throughout the nation. There are plans to build at least twenty more. Several of these facilities are planned for college campuses that are located in densely populated areas. While scientists carry on top secret research within the confines of the labs, the people in nearby communities have no idea what deadly poisons are being created so close to home. Terrorists, however, will be motivated to break into these facilities or target them with weapons of mass destruction. Top secret government facilities have a long history of spills, accidents, hazardous waste dumping, and gross mismanagement. Bioweapons labs should not be located on college campuses or in populated areas where the general public will be endangered.

President George W. Bush's [multibillion-dollar] plan to build laboratories across America to study deadly biological weapons has run into trouble with citizens in many parts of the country, evoking fears of spreading disease, attracting terrorist attacks and turning residential neighborhoods into government security zones.

In a two-month investigation [in 2003], United Press International [UPI] found roughly 20 existing high-level biodefense labs and proposals or plans to double that number through new construction and upgrades. These new facilities—many of them to be located in densely populated cities, on college campuses and residential neighborhoods—would study some of the world's most dangerous pathogens.

"We have a need for a tremendous amount of capacity," said Dr. Maureen McCarthy, acting director for the Office of Research and Development for the Science and Technology Directorate within the Department of Homeland Security. She said the recently adopted model for testing vaccines requires results in two types of animals. As a result of this, and the greater push to find countermeasures for bioweapons, the nation needs more and larger laboratories.

> As university officials were trying to reassure the townspeople no deadly microbes would be let loose, a monkey escaped from the primate center that would supply test animals for the lab's experiments.

Citizens and political action groups charge, however, that secrecy shrouds many of the projects and it has been difficult to find out what pathogens will be studied and whether the danger to humans and the environment around the laboratories has been fully considered.

In Davis, California, the city council refused to approve the biodefense lab plans of the University of California [in Davis], saying bringing such a lab to the town was too divisive. Citizen groups said the lab would bring deadly pathogens to Davis and they questioned safety measures. They asserted the facility would make the town a target for terrorists and bring national security restrictions to a campus with 22,000 undergraduates.

Just as university officials were trying to reassure the towns-people no deadly microbes would be let loose, a monkey escaped from the primate center that would supply test animals for the lab's experiments. The monkey has never been found and the incident heightened fear lab safety measures could be breached.

Some 3,000 miles from Davis, the Boston University Medical Center [BUMC] is seeking federal grants to build a major biodefense laboratory in Boston's densely populated and racially charged South End. Opposition groups contend people in the neighborhood have not been given a full picture of the lab's dangers.

> **❝ Though some planned labs are on military bases and in remote areas, many are being considered at universities and hospitals located near or in the center of dense urban areas. ❞**

On Long Island, N.Y., public citizens groups sharply oppose plans for defense research into biological weapons on Plum Island, a government facility 1.5 miles offshore of their communities and near Boston and New York.

The two Democratic New York senators, Hillary Clinton and Charles Schumer, have moved to stop the Homeland Security Department from upgrading the lab so diseases such as highly contagious, untreatable hemorrhagic fevers cannot be studied there. Homeland officials told Clinton the lab will not be upgraded to the highest level of [biological threat] containment, but area groups are still opposed to bioterrorism experiments there.

The Department of Energy is planning to build a biological defense lab at [the] Lawrence Livermore [National Laboratory] nuclear weapons facility despite the fact it would be located near San Francisco—in a well-known earthquake area—with 7 million people living within a 50-mile radius. The Livermore lab has also been under severe criticism for security breaches, raising concerns about the safety of any new facility.

In Hamilton, Mont., citizens groups claim a National Institutes of Health [NIH] plan to build a biodefense lab there has been rushed without sufficient consideration of how to deal with a major disease outbreak or environmental damage. NIH has just completed a new environmental impact statement and more public hearings are planned.

The Utah State University at Logan backed off a plan to seek federal money to build a top security biodefense lab after meeting public resistance. Secret government chemical and biological warfare testing always has been sensitive in Utah, where the Army has maintained its main testing center for those weapons at the Dugway Proving Ground. Opposition from citizens, the state government and its congressional delegation prevented the Army from developing the same type of lab at Dugway in 1985.

Building Biodefense Laboratories

In the weeks after the terrorist attacks and anthrax deaths in New York, Washington and Florida in the fall of 2001, there were few limits on what the Bush administration and Congress were willing to do to fight terrorism. They reached for the ultimate weapon of the United States Government—money—proposing $10.6 billion for bioterrorism defense research, vaccines and treatments.

The Bush Administration also gave the departments of Defense, Energy, Agriculture and Health and Human Services which includes the Centers for Disease Control and Prevention, the Environmental Protection Agency, and later the Department of Homeland Security, money to build or upgrade biodefense labs.

[As of mid-2003] the federal government [had] not published a list of biodefense labs either existing or proposed. The Sunshine Project, a private arms control research center located in Austin, Texas and Hamburg Germany, said there are plans to build or upgrade some 35 high-security biodefense laboratories around the country. UPI identified some 20 existing biodefense labs and found proposals or plans to build or upgrade roughly another 20. Though some planned labs are on military bases and in remote areas, many are being considered at universities and hospitals located near or in the center of dense urban areas.

Lab safety is measured by the ability to contain deadly microbes. These labs would operate at the highest of four grades: Biosafety Level 3 [BSL 3] or Biosafety Level 4 [BSL 4]. The Biosafety Level 4 labs, like the one planned for Davis, will be conducting research on such deadly diseases as Marburg [dis-

44

ease], [hemorrhagic fever due to] Ebola [virus] and Lassa [hemorrhagic fever], for which there are no known cures and little public knowledge in the United States.

Marburg, a hemorrhagic fever, was described a few years ago in the book, *The Hot Zone*, by Richard Preston, as a complete disintegration of the body's system ending with unquenchable hemorrhaging of blood and fluid through almost every orifice.

The key role of these research laboratories is to produce small quantities of deadly biological pathogens, and use the agent to try to find vaccines or antidotes to their effects. In the course of this research, tens of thousands of animals, including nonhuman primates, will be given the diseases to study their effects. No animal will survive these tests. The care, security and safe disposal of the animals and their remains are major safety problems.

Though these high-safety-level research labs would likely assist in analyzing bioagents during a terrorist attack, that is not their focus. There is a separate, billion-dollar effort underway through the Department of Health and Human Services to develop a network of mostly lower-level labs to test samples during an attack.

More research and new labs are necessary, said experts, because the introduction of modern biotechnology over the past 25 years has potentially made biological weapons vastly more dangerous. Pathogens can be genetically engineered to be more stable, more virulent, more resistant to treatment and more difficult to detect.

> *The work in these laboratories is exceedingly dangerous to the scientists and potentially deadly to vast numbers of the population if the microbes were to get to the outside.*

The work in these laboratories is exceedingly dangerous to the scientists and potentially deadly to vast numbers of the population if the microbes were to get to the outside. Since most of the most lethal potential agents can be distributed through the air, the main approach to safety is preventing the germs and viruses from leaking out of the secure containers and rooms where scientists work with them.

Keeping the Public Uninformed

Consistently in interviews with UPI, citizens in such diverse locations as Davis, Boston . . . and Portland, Ore., said they were convinced the full dangers of the laboratories were not being made public.

But the public is not likely to be given much more information—even if there is a deadly leak at the lab down the street.

The law that helped set the entire lab expansion in motion—the Public Health Security and Bioterrorism Preparedness and Response Act of 2002—makes it illegal for a federal agency to reveal information about who has materials or what they are doing with them. Officials could not tell the citizens of Davis whether Marburg is being studied at the lab. This type of information has been specifically exempted from the Freedom of Information Act and anyone who releases such information is subject to fines of up to a quarter of a million dollars.

It is not just basic information being restricted. Also banned from release is information on security problems including the loss or theft of materials. Most important, no information is to be made available about the "release of a listed agent or toxin."

If dangerous materials were to leak from the lab or an infected animal escape, local residents—by law—[would] never be told.

Proponents of the labs told UPI that communities' fears are overblown. "We've built these laboratories in ways that they can be operated safely," said Ron Atlas, president of the American Society for Microbiology. "Is anything absolutely failsafe? Probably not. Do we have an excellent system of redundancy and safety? Yes. Do I think that Davis or other communities are at risk by having them? No. I think these are safe facilities."

One of the first proposals for funds to build a major, $200 million biological defense laboratory came from the University of California at Davis, one of the state's premier universities and research schools with nearly 30,000 students and 17,000 employees.

From many angles, UC Davis, as it is called locally, would have seemed a perfect candidate. The provost of the university, Dr. Virginia Hinshaw, is a virologist . . . and many of the world's most dangerous potential bioterrorism weapons are viruses. She is listed as the primary "investigator," the [highly qualified virus specialist] that would take charge of the NIH funded projects.

UC Davis also maintains a major primate center, with 4,279

apes, chimpanzees and monkeys, which are the primary test animals for the final stages of biodefense-related research.

According to a university spokesperson, Pat Bailey, the idea to bid for the giant lab grew out of a request from the California Department of Public Health, several years before the Sept. 11, 2001, terrorist attacks, to build a BSL 4 lab. The state has several BSL 3 labs, which could handle most bioterror weapons, but was seeking a facility able to handle exotic diseases like Ebola and other hemorrhagic fevers.

At first the university seemed to be getting support for the lab. Mayor Susan Boyd joined a university group visiting a similar laboratory in downtown Winnipeg, Canada (incidentally the only BSL 4 in Canada) and the city council voted its support.

But Samantha McCarthy, leader of a local activist group, told UPI that despite appearing to be open with the people of Davis, a 5,000-person town that abuts the university, school officials rushed public meetings and held back pertinent documents that would have made clear the dangers of such a lab.

When the university made public its application in February, it almost immediately ran into vocal and forceful resistance from faculty members, activist groups and the people of Davis.

The biggest issue was safety.

"UCD spokespersons represent the lab as 'safe,'" wrote Susan Mann, a history professor in a petition on behalf of faculty, "We would argue that it is not."

Mann said that the faculty members "do not doubt that the technologies and practices employed in the lab would be the most effective known to science at this date. We would be poor scholars of American history, however, if we did not heed the legacy of leaks, spills, fires, explosions, mismanagement, and accidents associated with UC's own Livermore and Los Alamos [New Mexico] laboratories."

History of Accidents

The University of California operates both the Livermore and Los Alamos National Laboratories, which handle top-secret research on nuclear weapons. A Department of Energy Inspector General's report released at almost the same time the application for the Davis laboratory went to Washington charged that $1 million in equipment has been missing at Los Alamos, including 365 computers. . . .

UC Davis tried to distance itself from these problems, but

citizen groups found it had filed an application for one of the "Research Centers of Excellence," which names Lawrence Livermore as a partner in bioterrorism research. The "Centers of Excellence" are groupings of researchers and institutions in 10 different regions of the country that will take on specific biodefense research projects.

Just as the debate over leaks and safety was heating up, a 2-year-old female Rhesus macaque monkey about 20 inches high and weighing 4.4 pounds escaped from UC Davis's primate center. The primate center is where the test animals would come from for the lab and one of the things that recommended Davis to NIH. But if a monkey who had been given a deadly disease escaped, it could spread the pathogen to animals and humans. Bailey said the monkey was scheduled for the breeding center and had been certified as having no diseases; nevertheless, the animal has never been found. Bailey claimed that, though monkeys go missing in the center several times a year, this is the first one in 40 years that got off the premises. It is presumed to have died in a sewer outlet.

> "While limits on public knowledge may be necessary to combat bioterrorism, they are incompatible with the spirit of open intellectual exchange."

Another professor, Miriam Wells, of the Department of Human and Community Development, sharply challenged the university's assertion that the work at the lab would be controlled by the university and bioterrorism research would be but a sidelight.

In a detailed point-by-point review of NIH and university documents, Wells concluded "it is almost certain that classified research would be conducted at this national biocontainment laboratory. The nature of university policy, the stated purpose and governance structure of the lab, the exigencies of operational funding, NIH's planned collaboration with the Department of Defense and our direct communication with NIH, all point to the likelihood of classified research."

The nature of what the lab would be used for concerned many faculty members "greatly."

"While limits on public knowledge may be necessary to combat bioterrorism, they are incompatible with the spirit of open intellectual exchange on which a public institution of higher education such as [UC Davis] is based," Wells wrote.

Citizen Support Disappears in Davis

By late February [2003], public support for the lab in Davis had largely disappeared and on the 26th the members of the City Council voted to reverse their original support and send a letter to Hinshaw over the signature of the mayor, Susan Boyd.

"Many of our citizens are deeply concerned about potential negative consequences of the facility on the UC Davis campus. These concerns include, but are not limited to those of health and safety issues," wrote Boyd. The town could not support the application, the letter said because the matter had become too divisive.

The site chosen by UC Davis is on the campus, not in Davis, so the university does not need the town's permission to continue. The loss of the town's support, however, was politically devastating.

McCarthy said that she believed real estate people in the Davis area became worried the publicity about the danger of becoming a terrorist target or facing a bioweapon leak would stop people from settling in this growing residential community.

In early May, as if to bear this out, the Davis Chamber of Commerce and the Davis City Council received two mysterious letters postmarked Brazil with what police called "unknown particles" in them. The FBI tested the particles and found nothing harmful. It is investigating the incident.

But McCarthy blamed it on the lab project. "Here is Davis now on the map and somebody in Brazil sends letters! Of course we'd be a terrorist target!"

UC Davis wrote to NIH and asked if it could amend its application for a new site. In April it received a letter from Mary Kirker, an NIH grants management officer, saying that it would have to stick to the site applied for.

Bailey told UPI that if the university received the grant, it would build the lab over public objections.

The Boston University Medical Center [BUMC] announced earlier this year it "plans to establish a National Center for Emerging Infectious Diseases and Biodefense" at BioSquare in the university's medical campus in Boston's South End. The university applied, like Davis, for a grant from NIH to construct the facility.

"There will be significant community support for this project," the announcement said, adding Boston's popular, three-term mayor, Thomas Menino had "indicated his support."

BUMC said it commissioned a poll of the Boston community "that indicated a majority of Boston voters are favorable to having a National Biocontainment Laboratory in Boston." According to the news release, "after they heard the details of the proposal to locate such a facility in Boston, 59 percent in BUMC's surrounding neighborhood were favorable to having it located at the proposed site.

But last week, a group of neighborhood organizations and individuals, including a member of the city council and a state representative, issued a statement saying BUMC has given little or no information on what the laboratory would actually do.

In a letter to the NIH asking to forestall any action on BUMC's proposal, the group said that "very little information" was "provided to the public about the proposed activities and potential threats that they may pose to our health and safety." There were one million people living within a 10-mile radius of the proposed lab that "would be put at risk," they asserted.

The group also said they cannot determine from what BUMC has told them whether recombinant DNA technology will be used at the laboratory. They said such a process was barred by Boston regulation in 1994 and the regulation is still in force.

"Given what we know about these types of facilities," the group said, "we do not want it here."

Ellen Berlin, the director of corporate communications for the Boston University Medical Center, said the proposed BSL 4 laboratory would not be doing recombinant DNA as local groups charged and despite their opposition, the university argues it has the support of Bostonians.

7

The U.S. Government's Biological Threat Assessment Policies Could Fuel a Biological Arms Race

Jonathan B. Tucker

Jonathan B. Tucker is a senior researcher at the Center for Nonproliferation Studies, an organization that studies ways to combat the spread of weapons of mass destruction.

In an effort to prevent bioterrorism, the Bush administration is spending billions on research that may entail the creation and study of genetically engineered pathogens. The rationale for such a policy—to stay one step ahead of terrorists who might attack with genetically modified biological agents that are resistant or immune to antibiotics and vaccines—is flawed. It is highly unlikely that terrorists have access to or knowledge about the expensive and complicated equipment used in genetic engineering. In addition, the prospect that genetically altered pathogens may be purposely created in the United States causes other nations to become concerned that the deadly agents might be used against them. Fearing a U.S. attack, nations such as North Korea and Iran might well institute their own programs to weaponize genetically altered pathogens. Meanwhile, information gleaned in laboratories could be stolen by terrorists or

Jonathan B. Tucker, "Biological Threat Assessment: Is the Cure Worse than the Disease?" *Arms Control Today*, October 2004, pp. 13–19. Copyright © 2004 by the Arms Control Association. Reproduced by permission.

purposely given to them. In announcing a policy that authorizes, even under tightly controlled conditions, the creation of new and ever more deadly pathogens, the United States is fueling a bioweapons arms race.

In the . . . years since the September 11 [2001] terrorist attacks and the subsequent mailings of anthrax bacterial spores, federal spending to protect the U.S. civilian population against biological terrorism has soared more than 18-fold. For the 2005 fiscal year, the Bush administration . . . requested about $7.6 billion for civilian biodefense, up from $414 million at the time of the 2001 attacks.

Several federal agencies are involved in biodefense research and development (R & D), and the huge increase in funding from the National Institutes of Health for work on "select agents," or pathogens and toxins of bioterrorism concern, has attracted thousands of academic scientists.

> *The administration's biodefense research agenda credits terrorists with having cutting-edge technological capabilities that they do not currently possess nor are likely to acquire anytime soon.*

Of growing concern to U.S. biodefense officials is the possibility that rapid advances in genetic engineering and the study of pathogenesis (the molecular mechanisms by which microbes cause disease) could enable hostile states or terrorists to create "improved" biowarfare agents with greater lethality, environmental stability, difficulty of detection, and resistance to existing drugs and vaccines. It is known, for example, that the Soviet biological weapons program did extensive exploratory work on genetically engineered pathogens. The Bush administration's response to this concern has been to place a greater emphasis on "science-based threat assessment," which involves the laboratory development and study of offensive biological weapons agents in order to guide the development of countermeasures. This approach is highly problematic, however, because it could undermine the ban on offensive development enshrined in the Biological Weapons Convention (BWC) and end up worsening the very dangers that the U.S. government seeks to reduce.

Biological Threat Assessment—
Weighing the Risks

The Bush administration contends that science-based threat assessment is needed to shorten the time between the discovery of new bioterrorist threats, such as pathogens engineered to be resistant to multiple antibiotics, and the development of medical countermeasures, such as vaccines and therapeutic drugs. This rationale is flawed, however, for three reasons.

First, the administration's biodefense research agenda credits terrorists with having cutting-edge technological capabilities that they do not currently possess nor are likely to acquire anytime soon. Information in the public domain suggests that although some al Qaeda terrorists are pursuing biological weapons, these efforts are technically rudimentary and limited to standard agents such as the anthrax bacterium and ricin, a widely available plant toxin. Assistance from a country with an advanced biological weapons program may be theoretically possible, but no state has ever transferred weaponized agents to terrorists, and the risks of retaliation and loss of control make this scenario unlikely. Although more sophisticated bioterrorist threats may emerge someday from the application of modern biotechnology, they are unlikely to materialize for several years.

> *Threat-assessment activities that a country pursues for defensive purposes may be perceived as offensive, particularly if those studies involve the genetic modification of pathogens to enhance their harmful properties.*

Second, prospective threat-assessment studies involving the creation of hypothetical pathogens are of limited value because of the difficulty of correctly predicting technological innovations by states or terrorist organizations. Distortions such as "mirror-imaging"—the belief that an adversary would approach a technical problem in the same way as the person doing the analysis—make such efforts a deeply flawed basis for the development of effective countermeasures.

Third, by blurring the already hazy line between offensive and defensive biological R & D, science-based threat assessment raises suspicions about U.S. compliance with the BWC and fosters a "biological security dilemma" that could lead to a new biological arms race. At the same time, the novel pathogens and related know-how generated by threat-assessment work could be stolen or diverted for malicious purposes, exacerbating the threat of bioterrorism.

Current Threat-Assessment Activities

Although biological threat-assessment studies have been under way for several years, they have received a major boost under the Bush administration. On April 21 [2004], after a 10-month policy review of national biodefense programs, President George W. Bush signed Homeland Security Presidential Directive 10 (HSPD-10). In addition to allocating roles and responsibilities among various federal agencies, this directive requires the Department of Homeland Security (DHS) to conduct a national risk assessment of new biological threats every two years and a "net assessment" of biodefense effectiveness and vulnerabilities every four years. Under HSPD-10, significant resources will be devoted to projecting future threats, not just addressing current ones. According to an unclassified summary of the directive, the U.S. government is "continuing to develop more forward-looking analyses, to include Red Teaming efforts, to understand new scientific trends that may be exploited by our adversaries to develop biological weapons and to help position intelligence collectors ahead of the problem."

The expression "Red Teaming" dates back to the Cold War, when "red" symbolized the Soviet Union and its Warsaw Pact allies; the term now refers to any simulation involving the actions of a hostile country or subnational group. In the biodefense context, Red Teaming covers a variety of activities including scenario writing and paper studies, computer modeling of hypothetical biological attacks, and the development and testing of novel pathogens and weaponization techniques in the laboratory in order to guide the preparation of defenses.

To expand U.S. government capabilities in the field of biological threat assessment, DHS recently established a new multiagency organization called the National Biodefense Analysis and Countermeasures Center (NBACC), headquartered at Fort Detrick, Maryland. NBACC comprises four specialized centers, including a Biothreat Characterization Center whose mission is to "conduct science-based comprehensive risk assessments to anticipate, prevent, and respond to and recover from an attack." The biothreat characterization program at NBACC will explore how bioterrorists might use genetic engineering and other advanced technologies to make viruses or bacteria more deadly or contagious.

In [a] published interview, Colonel Gerald W. Parker, director of the Science-Based Threat Analysis and Response Program Office at DHS, explained that the laboratory component of threat characterization "will be focused on addressing high-priority information gaps in either understanding the threat or our vulnerabilities." When asked if NBACC would conduct exploratory research on genetically engineered pathogens, Parker replied, "We will not be intentionally enhancing pathogenicity of organisms to do 'what-if' type studies. . . . [But] if there is information either in the classified or open literature, and it is validated information, that indicates that somebody may have [enhanced pathogenicity], and that we believe indicates that we might have a vulnerability in our defensive posture, we may have to, in fact, evaluate the technical feasibility and the vulnerability of our countermeasures."

The Biological Security Dilemma

Even if, as Parker asserts, threat-assessment studies at NBACC involving the creation of genetically modified pathogens will be carried out only in response to "validated" intelligence that a state or terrorist organization has already done so, other countries may perceive such efforts as a cover for illicit, offensively oriented activities. The reason is that the distinction between defensive and offensive biological R & D is largely a matter of intent, giving rise to a "security dilemma" in which efforts by some states to enhance their biological security inadvertently undermine the security of others. Because intent is so hard to judge reliably, states tend to err on the side of caution by reacting to the capabilities, rather than the stated intentions, of potential adversaries. As a result, threat-assessment activities that a country pursues for defensive purposes may be perceived as offensive, particularly if those studies involve the genetic modification of pathogens to enhance their harmful properties.

Although the Bush administration has expressed concern about alleged biological weapons development activities in North Korea, Syria, Iran, and Cuba, it appears to have a blind spot with regard to how its own biological threat-assessment efforts are perceived abroad. Rival nations, fearing that the U.S.

exploration of emerging biological weapons threats could generate scientific breakthroughs that would put them at a strategic disadvantage, may decide to pursue or expand similar activities. Even if these programs are initially defensive in orientation, they could acquire a momentum of their own that eventually pushes them over the line into the offensive realm.

> *The expanded pool of researchers currently engaged in biological threat-assessment studies could well include a few spies, terrorist sympathizers, or sociopaths.*

The biological security dilemma has been inadvertently deepened by policies that the United States adopted after the September 11 attacks to tighten physical security and access controls at laboratories that possess, store, or transfer select agents. Although these new regulations aim to prevent the theft or diversion of dangerous pathogens and toxins for malicious purposes, they have had the undesirable side effect of reducing the transparency of biodefense R & D at a time when greater openness is needed to reassure outsiders of the benign intent behind such activities. Moreover, since the mid-1990s, the U.S. government has conducted an unknown number of classified threat-assessment studies, three of which were reported by *The New York Times* in September 2001. The stated rationale for classification is to prevent terrorists from learning about and exploiting U.S. vulnerabilities to biological attack, but secrecy has the pernicious effect of increasing suspicions about U.S. intentions and worsening the security dilemma.

The most serious risk associated with science-based threat assessment is that the novel pathogens and information it generates could leak out to rogue states and terrorists. To prevent such proliferation, the United States will have to impose even more stringent security measures. Yet history suggests that the greatest risk of leakage does not come from terrorists breaking into a secure laboratory from the outside, but rather from trusted insiders within the biodefense community who decide, for various motives, to divert sensitive materials or information for sale or malicious use.

The expanded pool of researchers currently engaged in bi-

56

ological threat-assessment studies could well include a few spies, terrorist sympathizers, or sociopaths. Moreover, because a pathogen culture can be smuggled out of a laboratory in a small, easily concealable plastic vial, the odds of getting caught are fairly low. Security background checks on scientists working with select agents can reduce the threat of diversion but not eliminate it, as suggested by the cases of CIA or FBI insiders who became spies, such as Aldridge Ames and Robert Hanssen. Indeed, although the perpetrator of the mailings of anthrax bacterial spores in the fall of 2001 remains unknown, the technical expertise needed to prepare the highly refined material points to someone with experience inside the biodefense research complex.

Thus, rather than enhancing U.S. national security, science-based threat-assessment projects involving the development of novel pathogens are likely to create a vicious circle that ends up worsening the problems of biological warfare and bioterrorism. Prospective threat assessment entails two simultaneous risks: (1) developing dangerous new technologies that will leak out to proliferators and terrorists and create a self-fulfilling prophecy, and (2) undermining the norms in the BWC and provoking a biological arms race at the state level, even if the countries involved merely seek to anticipate and counter offensive developments by potential adversaries.

Breaking Out of the Vicious Circle

In order to break out of the vicious circle created by the biological security dilemma, the United States should reduce its current emphasis on science-based threat assessment and pursue . . . strategies to build confidence in the strictly peaceful nature of its biodefense program.

The U.S. government should promote greater international transparency [accessibility of information] in biodefense R & D by including in its annual confidence-building measure (CBM) declarations under the BWC a comprehensive list of all of its biodefense activities, including classified projects, while omitting sensitive technical details that could assist proliferators or terrorists. (The fact that the United States had not declared the three secret threat-assessment studies uncovered by *The New York Times* suggested to some that it wished to avoid international scrutiny of legally dubious biodefense work. In those rare cases where the risk of proliferation warrants classification,

U.S. officials should explain why the experiments were done and provide a clear rationale for the limits on transparency. As a rule, however, openness should be considered the default condition, and any U.S. government agency seeking to classify specific biodefense projects or activities should be required to justify the need for secrecy.

A second approach to building confidence would be for the United States to conduct biological threat-assessment studies jointly with other countries. NATO [North Atlantic Treaty Organization] allies such as Canada, France, Germany, and the United Kingdom (as well as non-NATO countries such as Sweden) have advanced biodefense programs.

> *The most effective way for the United States to build international confidence in the peaceful nature of its biodefense program would be for the president to [renounce] the prospective development of genetically modified microorganisms.*

Although the U.S. government conducts some joint R & D with allies, these efforts are currently pursued on an ad hoc basis. Integrating Canada, the European Union, and the United States into a formal system of collaborative biodefense R & D that includes effective oversight would give the international community greater confidence that Washington is not pursuing a unilateral path in this highly sensitive area and that its biodefense R & D program is fully compliant with the BWC.

Russia is also a potential U.S. partner in the biodefense field because of the large number of former bioweapons scientists and facilities remaining from the Soviet biowarfare program and the existence of several areas in which the two countries have complementary expertise and pathogen strain collections. To date, however, U.S.-Russian biodefense collaboration has been undermined by Moscow's refusal to share a genetically modified strain of the anthrax bacterium and the fact that biodefense facilities under the control of the Russian Ministry of Defense remain off-limits to Western scientists. These issues will have to be resolved before joint U.S.-Russian R & D can become a source of greater international confidence in the BWC compliance of both countries.

A third approach to breaking out of the vicious circle is to improve the domestic oversight of biological threat assessment. In October 2003, the National Research Council of the U.S. National Academy of Sciences released the report of an expert panel chaired by Dr. Gerald R. Fink on preventing the malicious application of "dual-use" research in the life sciences. This report identified seven types of experiments that could result in information with a potential for misuse, including the genetic modification of pathogens to explore the mechanisms by which microbes cause disease. The Fink committee recommended the creation of a voluntary system for reviewing the security implications of federally funded biological research at the proposal stage. Such oversight would be performed at the local level by Institutional Biosafety Committees and at the national level by a new oversight board made up of scientists and security experts. . . .

Perhaps the most effective way for the United States to build international confidence in the peaceful nature of its biodefense program would be for the president to make a public statement renouncing the prospective development of genetically modified microorganisms with increased pathogenicity for threat-assessment purposes and urging all other countries to follow suit. As noted above, because the utility of prospective studies of genetically modified pathogens is severely limited by mirror-imaging and other sources of error, abandoning such studies would entail little risk to U.S. national security. On rare occasions, it may be necessary to test the efficacy of standard drugs or vaccines against genetically engineered pathogens that have already been developed by other countries. In these cases, the study should require a special authorization from the president following a careful interagency review to ensure that the proposed work complies with the letter as well as the spirit of the BWC.

To enforce the proposed unilateral ban on the prospective development of new pathogens with increased pathogenicity, the president should encourage scientists within the biodefense community to "blow the whistle" if they become aware of unauthorized studies that violate this policy, regardless of whether the work is being conducted in an academic setting or in a top-secret government laboratory. Confidential reporting channels and legal protections should also be established to shield scientists who expose illicit activities. To bolster the norm of professional responsibility further, scientists working in federal biodefense programs should be required to sign a code of conduct, similar to the Hippocratic oath, that precludes them from deliberately developing agents with enhanced pathogenicity or other harmful properties and requires them to report any deviations from this norm. . . .

These practical steps are needed to prevent the Bush administration's growing emphasis on science-based threat assessment from increasing biological weapons proliferation risks, exacerbating the security dilemma, weakening the BWC, and drawing the United States into a dangerous biological arms race. It is time to break the vicious circle before it starts.

8

The U.S. Government's Biological Threat Assessment Policies Will Protect Americans

George W. Bush

George W. Bush is the forty-third president of the United States.

Bioterrorism is one of the gravest dangers facing the United States in the twenty-first century. America's enemies can threaten the well-being of the entire nation with nothing more than a single vial of biological material. With this peril looming, the federal government has instituted the Biodefense for the 21st Century program to explore every possible means of preventing such an attack or, failing that, responding to it. Billions of dollars have been directed to programs that address such aspects of the problem as stemming proliferation of biological pathogens, protecting Americans from bioterrorism, and minimizing harm if an attack occurs. The United States is reaching out to the international community as well as coordinating private, local, and state efforts to confront the new threat of biological weapons. A bioterrorist attack can cause deaths, long-term disabilities, economic disruption, and widespread panic. Under the Biodefense for the 21st Century program, the formidable capabilities of American science

George W. Bush, "Biodefense for the 21st Century," www.whitehouse.gov, April 28, 2004.

and intelligence, along with public health and law enforcement agencies, are aligned to mount a credible defense against threats of this kind.

B iological weapons in the possession of hostile states or terrorists pose unique and grave threats to the safety and security of the United States and our allies.

Biological weapons attacks could cause catastrophic harm. They could inflict widespread injury and result in massive casualties and economic disruption. Bioterror attacks could mimic naturally occurring disease, potentially delaying recognition of an attack and creating uncertainty about whether one has even occurred. An attacker may thus believe that he could escape identification and capture or retaliation.

Biological weapons attacks could be mounted either inside or outside the United States and, because some biological weapons agents are contagious, the effects of an initial attack could spread widely. Disease outbreaks, whether natural or deliberate, respect no geographic or political borders.

The United States has pursued aggressively a broad range of programs and capabilities to confront the biological weapons threat.

Preventing and controlling future biological weapons threats will be even more challenging. Advances in biotechnology and life sciences—including the spread of expertise to create modified or novel organisms—present the prospect of new toxins, live agents, and bioregulators that would require new detection methods, preventive measures, and treatments. These trends increase the risk for surprise. Anticipating such threats through intelligence efforts is made more difficult by the dual-use nature of biological technologies and infrastructure, and the likelihood that adversaries will use denial and deception to conceal their illicit activities.

The stakes could not be higher for our Nation. Attacks with biological weapons could:
 • Cause catastrophic numbers of acute casualties, long-term disease and disability, psychological trauma, and mass panic;

- Disrupt critical sectors of our economy and the day-to-day lives of Americans; and
- Create cascading international effects by disrupting and damaging international trade relationships, potentially globalizing the impacts of an attack on United States soil.

A Critical Foundation

Fortunately, the United States possesses formidable capabilities to mount credible biodefenses. We have mobilized our unrivaled biomedical research infrastructure and expanded our international research relationships. In addition, we have an established medical and public health infrastructure that is being revitalized and expanded. These capabilities provide a critical foundation on which to build improved and comprehensive biodefenses.

The United States has pursued aggressively a broad range of programs and capabilities to confront the biological weapons threat. These actions, taken together, represent an extraordinary level of effort by any measure. Among our significant accomplishments, we have:

- Expanded international efforts to keep dangerous biological materials out of the hands of terrorists;
- Launched the Proliferation Security Initiative to stem the trafficking in weapons of mass destruction (WMD), including biological weapons;
- Established the BioWatch program, a network of environmental sensors to detect biological weapons attacks against major cities in the United States;
- Initiated new programs to secure and defend our agriculture and food systems against biological contamination;
- Increased funding for bioterrorism research within the Department of Health and Human Services by thirty-fold;
- Expanded the Strategic National Stockpile of medicines for treating victims of bioterror attacks, ensuring that the stockpile's "push packages" can be anywhere in the United States within 12 hours;
- Stockpiled enough smallpox vaccine for every American, and vaccinated over 450,000 members of the armed services;
- Launched and funded Project BioShield to speed the development and acquisition of new medical countermeasures against biological weapons;
- Provided Federal funds to improve the capacities of state

and local health systems to detect, diagnose, prevent, and respond to biological weapons attacks; and
- Worked with the international community to strengthen global, regional and national programs to prevent, detect, and respond to biological weapons attacks.

Building on these accomplishments, we conducted a comprehensive evaluation of our biological defense capabilities to identify future priorities and actions to support them. The results of that study provide a blueprint for our future biodefense program, Biodefense for the 21 Century, that fully integrates the sustained efforts of the national and homeland security, medical, public health, intelligence, diplomatic, and law enforcement communities.

Specific direction to departments and agencies to carry out this biodefense program is contained in a classified version of this directive.

Biodefense for the 21st Century

The United States will continue to use all means necessary to prevent, protect against, and mitigate biological weapons attacks perpetrated against our homeland and our global interests. Defending against biological weapons attacks requires us to further sharpen our policy, coordination, and planning to integrate the biodefense capabilities that reside at the Federal, state, local, and private sector levels. We must further strengthen the strong international dimension to our efforts, which seeks close international cooperation and coordination with friends and allies to maximize our capabilities for mutual defense against biological weapons threats.

While the public health philosophy of the 20th Century—emphasizing prevention—is ideal for addressing natural disease outbreaks, it is not sufficient to confront 21st Century threats where adversaries may use biological weapons agents as part of a long-term campaign of aggression and terror. Health care providers and public health officers are among our first lines of defense. Therefore, we are building on the progress [since 2001] to further improve the preparedness of our public health and medical systems to address current and future BW threats and to respond with greater speed and flexibility to multiple or repetitive attacks.

Private, local, and state capabilities are being augmented by and coordinated with Federal assets, to provide layered defenses against biological weapons attacks. These improvements will complement and enhance our defense against emerging or reemerging natural infectious diseases.

The traditional approach toward protecting agriculture, food, and water—focusing on the natural or unintentional introduction of a disease—also is being greatly strengthened by focused efforts to address current and anticipated future biological weapons threats that may be deliberate, multiple, and repetitive.

> **"** We must further strengthen the strong international dimension to our efforts, which seeks close international cooperation and coordination with friends and allies. **"**

Finally, we are continuing to adapt United States military forces to meet the biological weapons challenge. We have long recognized that adversaries may seek biological weapons to overcome our conventional strength and to deter us from responding to aggression. A demonstrated military capability to defend against biological weapons and other WMD strengthens our forward military presence in regions vital to United States security, promotes deterrence, and provides reassurance to critical friends and allies. The Department of Defense will continue to ensure that United States military forces can operate effectively in the face of biological weapons attacks, and that our troops and our critical domestic and overseas installations are effectively protected against such threats.

Pillars of Our Biodefense Program

The essential pillars of our national biodefense program are: Threat Awareness, Prevention and Protection, Surveillance and Detection, and Response and Recovery. . . .

National biodefense preparedness and response requires the involvement of a wide range of Federal departments and agencies. The Secretary of Homeland Security is the principal Federal official for domestic incident management and is responsible for coordinating domestic Federal operations to prepare for, respond to, and recover from biological weapons attacks. . . .

The Secretary of State is the principal Federal officer responsible for international terrorist incidents that take place outside the U.S. territory, including United States support for foreign consequence management and coordinates, as appropriate, with heads of other Federal departments and agencies, to effectively accomplish this mission. When requested by the Secretary of State, and approved by the Secretary of Defense, the Department of Defense will support United States foreign consequence management operations, as appropriate. . . .

[O]ur aims and objectives for further progress under each of the pillars of our national biodefense program [are as follows]:

Threat Awareness

Biological Warfare Related Intelligence

Timely, accurate, and relevant intelligence enables all aspects of our national biodefense program. Despite the inherent challenges of identifying and characterizing biological weapons programs and anticipating biological attacks, we are improving the intelligence community's ability to collect, analyze, and disseminate intelligence. We are increasing the resources dedicated to these missions and adopting more aggressive approaches for accomplishing them. Among our many initiatives, we are continuing to develop more forward-looking analyses, to include Red Teaming efforts [simulations of biological attacks for learning purposes], to understand new scientific trends that may be exploited by our adversaries to develop biological weapons and to help position intelligence collectors ahead of the problem. . . .

Anticipation of Future Threats

The proliferation of biological materials, technologies, and expertise increases the potential for adversaries to design a pathogen to evade our existing medical and non-medical countermeasures. To address this challenge, we are taking advantage of these same technologies to ensure that we can anticipate and prepare for the emergence of this threat. We are building the flexibility and speed to characterize such agents, assess existing defenses, and rapidly develop safe and effective countermeasures. In addition, we must guard against the spread of potentially infectious agents from beyond our borders. We are strengthening the ability of our medical, public health, agricultural, defense, law enforcement, diplomatic, environmental, and transportation infrastructures to recognize and confront such threats and to contain their impact. The Department of Health and Human Services, in coordination with other appropriate Federal departments and agencies, is working to ensure an integrated and focused national effort to anticipate and respond to emerging biological weapons threats.

Prevention and Protection

Proactive Prevention

Preventing biological weapons attacks is by far the most cost-effective approach to biodefense. Prevention requires the continuation and expansion of current multilateral initiatives to limit the access of agents, technology, and know-how to countries, groups, or individuals seeking to develop, produce, and use these agents.

To address this challenge, we are further enhancing diplomacy, arms control, law enforcement, multilateral export controls, and threat reduction assistance that impede adversaries seeking biological weapons capabilities. Federal departments and agencies with existing authorities will continue to expand threat reduction assistance programs aimed at preventing the proliferation of biological weapons expertise. We will continue to build international coalitions to support these efforts, encouraging increased political and financial support for nonproliferation and threat reduction programs. We will also continue to expand efforts to control access and use of pathogens to strengthen security and prevention.

> *The Department of Defense will continue to ensure that United States military forces can operate effectively in the face of biological weapons attacks.*

The *National Strategy to Combat Weapons of Mass Destruction*, released in December 2002, places special emphasis on the need for proactive steps to confront WMD threats. Consistent with this approach, we have improved and will further improve our ability to detect and destroy an adversary's biological weapons assets before they can be used. We are also further expanding existing capabilities to interdict enabling technologies and materials, including through the Proliferation Security Initiative. Additionally, we are working to improve supporting intelligence capabilities to provide timely and accurate information to support proactive prevention. . . .

Critical Infrastructure Protection

Protecting our critical infrastructure from the effects of biological weapons attacks is a priority. A biological weapons attack might deny us access to essential facilities and response capabilities. Therefore, we are working to improve the survivability and ensure the continuity and restoration of operations of critical infrastructure sectors following biological weapons attacks. Assessing the vulnerability of this infrastructure, particularly the medical, public health, food, water, energy, agricultural, and transportation sectors, is the focus of current efforts. The Department of Homeland Security, in coordination with other appropriate Federal departments and agencies, leads these efforts, which include developing and deploying biodetection technologies and decontamination methodologies.

Surveillance and Detection

Attack Warning

Early warning, detection, or recognition of biological weapons attacks to permit a timely response to mitigate their consequences is an essential component of biodefense. Through the President's [2004] biosurveillance initiative, the United States is working to develop an integrated and comprehensive attack warning system to rapidly recognize and characterize the dispersal of biological agents in human and animal populations, food, water, agriculture, and the environment. Creating a national bioawareness system will permit the recognition of a biological attack at the earliest possible moment and permit initiation of a robust response to prevent unnecessary loss of life, economic losses, and social disruption. Such a system will be built upon and reinforce existing Federal, state, local, and international surveillance systems. . . .

Attribution

Deterrence is the historical cornerstone of our defense, and attribution—the identification of the perpetrator as well as method of attack—forms the foundation upon which deterrence rests. Biological weapons, however, lend themselves to covert or clandestine attacks that could permit the perpetrator to remain anonymous.

We are enhancing our deterrence posture by improving attribution capabilities. We are improving our capability to perform technical forensic analysis and to assimilate all-source information to enable attribution assessments. We have created and designated the National Bioforensic Analysis Center of the National Biodefense Analysis and Countermeasure Center, under the Department of Homeland Security, as the lead Federal facility to conduct and facilitate the technical forensic analysis and interpretation of materials recovered following a biological attack in support of the appropriate lead Federal agency.

Response and Recovery

Once a biological weapons attack is detected, the speed and coordination of the Federal, state, local, private sector, and international response will be critical in mitigating the lethal, medical, psychological, and economic consequences of such attacks. Responses to biological weapons attacks depend on pre-attack planning and preparedness, capabilities to treat casualties, risk communications, physical control measures, medical countermeasures, and decontamination capabilities. . . .

> *We are strengthening the ability of our medical, public health, agricultural, defense, law enforcement, diplomatic, environmental, and transportation infrastructures to recognize and confront such threats and to contain their impact.*

Mass Casualty Care

Following a biological weapons attack, all necessary means must be rapidly brought to bear to prevent loss of life, illness, psychological trauma, and to contain the spread of potentially contagious diseases. Provision of timely preventive treatments such as antibiotics or vaccines saves lives, protects scarce medical capabilities, preserves social order, and is cost effective.

The Administration is working closely with state and local public health officials to strengthen plans to swiftly distribute needed medical countermeasures. Moreover, we are working to expand and, where needed, create new Federal, state, and local medical and public health capabilities for all-hazard mass casualty care. . . .

Risk Communication

Timely communications with the general public and the medical and public health communities can significantly influence the success of response efforts, including health- and life-sustaining interventions. Efforts will be made to develop communication strategies, plans, products, and channels to reach all segments of our society, including those with physical or language limitations. These efforts will ensure timely domestic and international dissemination of information that educates and reassures the general public and relevant professional sectors before, during, and after an attack or other public health emergency.

The Department of Homeland Security, in coordination with other appropriate Federal departments and agencies, is developing comprehensive coordinated risk communication strategies to facilitate emergency preparedness for biological weapons attacks. This includes travel and citizen advisories, international coordination and communication, and response and recovery communications in the event of a large-scale biological attack.

Medical Countermeasure Development

Development and deployment of safe, effective medical countermeasures against biological weapons agents of concern remains an urgent priority. The National Institutes of Health (NIH), under the direction of the Department of Health and Human Services, is working with the Department of Homeland Security, the Department of Defense, and other agencies to shape and execute an aggressive research program to develop better medical countermeasures. NIH's work increasingly will reflect the potential for novel or genetically engineered biological weapons agents and possible scenarios that require providing broad-spectrum coverage against a range of possible biological threats to prevent illness even after exposure. Additionally, we have begun construction of new labs. We are striving to assure the nation has the infrastructure required to test and evaluate existing, proposed, or promising countermeasures, assess their safety and effectiveness, expedite their development, and ensure rapid licensure.

The Department of Health and Human Services, in coordination with other appropriate Federal departments and agencies, will continue to ensure the development and availability of sufficient quantities of safe and efficacious medical countermeasures to mitigate illness and death in the event of a biological weapons attack.

Decontamination

Recovering from a biological weapons attack may require significant decontamination and remediation activities. We are working to improve Federal capabilities to support states and localities in their efforts to rapidly assess, decontaminate, and return to pre-attack activities, and are developing standards and protocols for the most effective approaches for these activities.

9

A Comprehensive Vaccination Program Would Mitigate the Consequences of a Bioterrorist Attack

Michael Scardaville

Michael Scardaville is policy analyst for homeland security in the Kathryn and Shelby Cullom Davis Institute for International Studies at the Heritage Foundation, a conservative think tank.

Terrorists may use smallpox as a weapon against the United States. A smallpox attack against American civilians or military personnel could be disastrous. However, a comprehensive nationwide strategy to vaccinate health care professionals, military personnel, and first responders, as well as volunteers from the general public, would prevent such a tragedy. While serious complications may result from the use of the smallpox vaccine, a mass vaccination campaign would neutralize the threat of a terrorist smallpox attack. Terrorists who have declared war on the United States are on the lookout for areas in which Americans are vulnerable, and widespread lack of immunity to smallpox is a matter of common knowledge. It is central to the national security of the United States that a smallpox vaccination program be instituted immediately.

Michael Scardaville, "Public Health and National Security Planning: The Case for Voluntary Smallpox Vaccination," *Heritage Foundation Backgrounder*, December 6, 2002.

Vaccinating the American public against smallpox is no longer just a public health issue. In light of . . . statements attributed to [terrorist group] al-Qaeda leader Osama bin Laden, it has become a national security matter. Mounting concerns about new terrorist attacks, including biological attacks on American civilians, have intensified the debate among policy-makers and public health officials over how best to prepare for a smallpox attack, either with preemptive or post-attack vaccinations. Even a localized attack on non-immunized Americans could result in the deaths of a million or more people nationally. A comprehensive strategy is needed.

To protect Americans in the nearest possible term from such terrorism, the federal government should:

- carry through on plans to vaccinate essential military personnel immediately;
- urge states to vaccinate all first responders and public health officials essential to their state and local response plans; and
- make the vaccine available to the general public for voluntary inoculations following a broad campaign of education.

From a national security perspective, preemptive but voluntary smallpox vaccinations for the general public—along with a more comprehensive vaccination program for military personnel and critical first responders—makes the most sense. Voluntary vaccinations would help reduce the spread of the disease were it used as a weapon, improve the ability of the public health sector to treat those infected from an attack, reduce panic during a crisis, and provide a reasonable deterrent to the use of smallpox by terrorists.

While the vaccine does pose some risks, these are offset by the growing threat and the government's responsibility to ensure Americans' well-being. Moreover, compared with a mandatory vaccination regime, a voluntary vaccination program would respect an individual's right to choose whether or not to absorb the risks of inoculation.

Assessing the Risks

Smallpox is an extremely contagious disease once a victim begins to show symptoms—usually seven to 17 days after exposure. Historically, it has a fatality rate of approximately 30 percent. An attack against an unprotected population, therefore, could spread rapidly and have dire consequences. However, statistics also predict that, absent an attack, approximately 300 people would die in a mass inoculation program.

Knowing this, policymakers must decide whether to vaccinate everyone before an attack or wait until after an attack to begin the vaccinations. While some officials are considering a mandatory inoculation program, a voluntary preemptive program that respects the right of each person to decide whether to absorb the risk associated with the vaccine rather than the risk of contracting smallpox would be far more effective. It would promote national preparedness by reducing the numbers that would need to be vaccinated should an attack occur and also address important liability concerns that could discourage the vaccine's manufacturers.

The Use of Smallpox as a Bioweapon

In 1980, the World Health Organization (WHO) declared that smallpox had been eradicated as a naturally occurring disease, with the last known case having occurred in Somalia in 1977. Currently, there are only two WHO-approved and inspected repositories of the live virus: the Centers for Disease Control and Prevention (CDC) in Atlanta and Vector Laboratories in Russia. All other nations holding stores of the virus were directed to destroy them or send them to one of these facilities.

Nevertheless, clandestine stockpiles are believed to exist in states such as Iraq and Iran that have worrisome ties to terrorist organizations. Further, the former Soviet Union is suspected of experimenting with weaponizing the smallpox virus during the 1980s in violation of international agreements. While those stocks are believed to have been destroyed, experience has shown that Soviet (and early post-Soviet Russian) security at its weapons of mass destruction (WMD) research and storage facilities was questionable at best; stocks of the virus could have been smuggled out. As a result, it is very difficult to determine the extent of the threat today.

U.S. Vulnerability

Though the likelihood of a smallpox attack and the merits of different vaccination strategies are certainly open to debate, the potential consequences of an attack and the vulnerability of the U.S. population to an outbreak are not. American civilians have not been vaccinated against smallpox since 1972, and the Department of Defense stopped vaccinating troops in the 1980s (a new military vaccination program [was] being reviewed by the White House [in 2002]). As a result, those under 30 years of age—approximately 42 percent of the American population—are not likely to have been vaccinated; they would be highly susceptible to contracting smallpox in the event of an attack.

> **"** *Even a localized attack on non-immunized Americans could result in the deaths of a million or more people nationally.* **"**

Added to this concern is the fact that it is not known whether those vaccinated before 1972 retain any immunity to the disease. The lack of immunity would make the general population grossly vulnerable to the disease.

Hazards Associated with the Smallpox Vaccine

The smallpox vaccine also carries significant risks. Experience with the vaccination program in the United States prior to 1972 indicates that approximately one in every 1 million first-time recipients is likely to die from complications. Therefore, a complete vaccination of the U.S. population could cost 300 lives. Estimates of how many people would suffer from serious complications but not die vary dramatically from one in every 8,000 to one in every 67,000.

Opponents of vaccinating the general population in advance of an attack include the American Medical Association and other groups in the medical community. They typically cite two reasons for their opposition: the unknown nature of the threat and the risks associated with the vaccine. The logic behind their decision is twofold: (1) a belief that, without a better assessment of the threat, the potential loss of life (even if only a tiny fraction of the population) outweighs the benefits of vaccination and (2) concerns over the legal liability of the administering physicians as the distributors of the vaccine. They suggest limiting pre-incident vaccination to the military and those first responders who choose to receive it. The general population would be left vulnerable and would not receive treatment until after an attack.

But ignoring national security concerns and choosing a vaccination strategy based merely on public health concerns would leave the United States defenseless against an attack. Terrorists such as al-Qaeda operatives will look for any deficiencies in domestic preparedness and take advantage of them.

The CDC's Flawed Post-Attack Approach

Since the terrorist and anthrax attacks of 2001, the CDC and its parent agency, the U.S. Department of Health and Human Services, have undertaken significant efforts to ensure that . . . there will be enough smallpox vaccine available to inoculate every American. The policy procedure for implementing this objective is developing more slowly.

Initially, the CDC planned to rely only on a strategy known as ring vaccination, which helped to eliminate the natural occurrence of smallpox in the 1960s and 1970s. This strategy relies on tracking down all those who came into contact with the initial case (or cases) and vaccinating them within four days of the initial exposure.

> *Ignoring national security concerns and choosing a vaccination strategy based merely on public health concerns would leave the United States defenseless against an attack.*

Such an approach is poorly suited to combating a terrorist attack using smallpox, since hundreds or thousands of people would be infected during the initial release of the virus. In America's highly mobile society, those initially infected are likely to spread the disease over a very wide geographic area. Tracking down all those who have had contact with the original infected group would be a huge undertaking. Yale University Professor Edward Kaplan is among those who are pessimistic about using the ring vaccination strategy. Concerning the CDC plan, he said it would be "a fantasy to believe that the control of small natural outbreaks provides guidance for large bioterrorist attacks."

Further, much of the vital four-day window in which post-exposure vaccination is known to be effective in preventing illness would be absorbed by logistics. As recently as June of [2002], the CDC's Advisory Committee on Immunization Practices (ACIP), which developed the ring smallpox vaccination strategy, noted that only one lab in the nation (the CDC in Atlanta) is capable of confirming a case of smallpox and that such a determination can take between eight and 24 hours.

> *The CDC . . . should begin drafting a set of guidelines for distributing the vaccine to hospitals nationwide and for screening out prospective recipients at high risk of experiencing complications.*

Moreover, it will take 12 to 24 hours for the vaccine in the National Pharmaceutical Stockpile to reach its distribution points. Even if a first-generation case was sent promptly to the CDC in Atlanta for review, much of that crucial four-day vaccination window would be lost, and the ability to prevent the onslaught of second-generation cases would be less certain. . . .

The Value of Voluntary Vaccination for National Defense

After a smallpox attack, the difficulties associated with the ring vaccination program or CDC's crisis management approach to mass vaccinations could be greatly reduced if even a portion of those in the target area did not need to be vaccinated. Ensuring some degree of prior immunity among the population at large through preemptive and voluntary vaccinations would boost the public health sector's ability to stop the spread of the disease, since fewer people would be likely to contract and spread it. This also would mitigate the national (and potentially international) consequences of an attack.

Moreover, a voluntary vaccination program implemented during a non-crisis time would enable doctors to take more exacting measures. They would be better able to screen out patients at high risk for complications from the vaccine—for example, people with weakened immune systems or a history of skin problems, pregnant women, or children under one year of age. With the number of people who need vaccinations after an attack reduced, the risk of chaos also would fall, with fewer people rushing to hospitals to be treated, and the availability of adequate outpatient and follow-up care would rise.

A Plan for Action

The CDC should begin developing standards for voluntary vaccinations with the intent of instituting that strategy [as soon as possible] instead of focusing on how to vaccinate potentially millions of Americans after an attack. The CDC also should begin drafting a set of guidelines for distributing the vaccine to hospitals nationwide and for screening out prospective recipients at high risk of experiencing complications. And it should begin drafting standards for post-procedure care to reduce the likelihood of complications or further transmission.

The CDC also should develop an educational program on the risks associated with smallpox and the vaccine. This program should not encourage or discourage vaccination, but simply lay out the facts clearly so that each American can make an educated decision. The administering physicians should inform potential recipients of the risks involved, consistent with CDC's guidelines, and those who agree to the inoculation should sign a waiver noting that they understand the risks and accept responsibility for potential side effects.

Beyond these guidelines, the federal government should leave ultimate responsibility for the details of the distribution program with state and local authorities.

Inoculating Frontline Military Personnel

The Department of Defense reportedly plans to vaccinate approximately 500,000 of its 1.4 million active duty personnel, beginning with medical staff and followed by those troops likely to be deployed to the Middle East. Procedures for immunizing these frontline troops should continue as planned. The Defense Department should also plan to expand this program to vital National Guard personnel who would likely be called upon to assist civil authorities during a domestic smallpox attack.

Consideration must also be given to the fact that vulnerability among the nation's first responders directly affects the country's ability to respond to an attack. These professionals are likely to find themselves in close and more frequent contact with infected people in the event of attack. Every community, therefore, will need to have some first responders, particularly health care workers, who are immune to the disease already and can operate in an environment where the virus is abundant (such as secure areas of a hospital or other locations dedicated to the care of smallpox victims). But many first responder jobs will also be required in lower-risk areas. Consequently, a federally mandated, universal program for vaccinating all first responders, while beneficial, may not be necessary.

> *In a nation where trial attorneys view litigation as a mechanism for social activism, it is likely that financial compensation will be sought by some.*

Vaccination standards for first responders should therefore be left up to state and local agencies. The federal government should encourage the states and communities to vaccinate personnel deemed essential to the community's smallpox response plan, but it should allow the local authorities to determine who those personnel are and how to implement the vaccination requirement. First responders who are not essential to a community's smallpox response plan could participate in a voluntary program; they should not be required to be immunized as a condition of their first-responder position.

Dealing with Liability Concerns

The federal government should take action now to address the potential liability concerns of a vaccination program, but it should not assume responsibility for health decisions made by individuals. Public education will be crucial not only to reducing America's susceptibility to a smallpox attack, but also to addressing the liability concerns properly.

The Food and Drug Administration (FDA) has never approved the current supply of smallpox vaccine. Though the vaccine's risks and benefits are well-documented from its long use prior to 1972, it is currently being distributed under Investigational New Drug (IND) protocols designed to determine whether it is reasonably safe for initial use in humans. Nonetheless, in a nation where trial attorneys view litigation as a mechanism for social activism, it is likely that financial compensation will be sought by some of those who accept the vaccine and later become ill or by families of the small number of people who die as a result of complications. In a voluntary vaccination program that includes pretreatment education about the known risks and the degree of uncertainty of outcome, primary responsibility for the decision to take advantage of the smallpox vaccine should lie with the individuals who seek it. . . .

Smallpox is not a known disease, and inoculating the entire population to avert the effects of a feared terrorist attack would expose far more people to the possibility of complications than do the current inoculations for other known diseases. A voluntary program using vaccines with well-established risks that allows each person to decide whether to expose himself or herself to those risks or remain at risk of contracting the disease itself in a bioterrorist attack is a better approach. To defer some of the potential costs of adverse reactions to the vaccine, people who choose the inoculation should seek health insurance to cover that risk. . . .

The Best Approach to Vaccinating America Against Smallpox

The federal government's responsibility rests in developing a vaccination program that protects the security and safety of the nation. The CDC [has had] enough vaccine for every American [since] the end of 2003. Combined with a well-prepared public health sector and a clear post-incident vaccination strategy, a voluntary preemptive vaccination program would mitigate the consequences of a terrorist attack by limiting the spread of the disease and reducing panic without trampling on the freedom of Americans to decide for themselves how best to protect themselves and their families. There are significant risks with the smallpox vaccine, but the risk of bioterrorism is rising, and Americans should be allowed to weigh all those risks as they relate to their own safety. . . .

From a national security perspective, a preemptive but voluntary smallpox vaccination program for the general public in addition to a more comprehensive vaccination of military personnel and first responders makes sense. Preemptive vaccinations administered in this manner would reduce the spread of the disease, improve the public health sector's ability to treat those at risk or infected after an attack, reduce panic and potential chaos during a crisis, and provide a reasonable deterrent to the use of smallpox by terrorists.

While the vaccine does pose some risk to Americans, these risks are offset by the growing threat of a smallpox attack and the government's need to protect the nation and the well-being of the population at large. In contrast to a mandatory vaccination regime, a voluntary vaccination program also respects an individual's right to choose.

10

Smallpox Vaccinations Pose Considerable Health Risks for Medical Personnel

Thomas May, Mark P. Aulisio, and Ross D. Silverman

Thomas May is director of graduate studies in bioethics at the Center for the Study of Bioethics, Medical College of Wisconsin. Mark P. Aulisio is director of the Clinical Ethics Program at MetroHealth Medical Center and director of the master's program in bioethics in Case Western Reserve University's Department of Bioethics. Ross D. Silverman teaches medical humanities at Southern Illinois University's School of Medicine.

In the weeks following the destruction of the World Trade Center on September 11, 2001, two senators and five media outlets received letters contaminated with the deadly anthrax bacteria. Five people who handled the mail died and new fears were expressed that a similar attack with smallpox might be imminent. Citing national security concerns, President George W. Bush suggested that more than a half million doctors, nurses, and other medical providers be inoculated with the smallpox vaccine. A majority of medical professionals, however, justifiably refused to be vaccinated and also refused to require their employees to be vaccinated. Smallpox is extremely difficult to use as a weapon of

Thomas May, Mark P. Aulisio, and Ross D. Silverman, "The Smallpox Vaccination of Health Care Workers," *Hastings Center Report*, vol. 33, September/October 2003. Copyright © 2003 by the Hastings Center. Reproduced by permission.

mass destruction, and complications associated with the use of the vaccine can include heart failure, encephalitis, and transmission of the disease to others. Health care professionals are not obligated to put their health, and perhaps their lives, at risk because of the rare chance that a mass smallpox attack might occur.

In early December 2002, President [George W.] Bush announced plans for the immediate vaccination of approximately 500,000 health care professionals against smallpox on a voluntary basis (as well as up to 500,000 military personnel on a mandatory basis). These health care professionals would act as smallpox response teams in the event of a terror attack using this agent, treating cases and administering vaccination to the general population. Within days of Bush's announcement, however, two prominent teaching hospitals refused to vaccinate their employees against smallpox, and several others were leaning toward similar refusal. In addition, several prominent medical associations expressed concerns about smallpox vaccination prior to an actual attack using this agent, including the American Medical Association, the American Academy of Family Physicians, and the American Academy of Pediatricians.

> *The smallpox vaccine is a 'live' vaccine that infects the recipient with a related virus. After being vaccinated, the recipient can spread this infection to others.*

An even bleaker picture emerged in an April 2003 report from the General Accounting Office [GAO] to the chairman of the U.S. Senate Committee on Governmental Affairs concerning the problems implementing the smallpox vaccination program. The report observed that hundreds of hospitals and thousands of health professionals have refused to participate in pre-event vaccination until liability and compensation issues have been resolved. Compensation is viewed as necessary because many will miss work or experience medical problems as the result of vaccination. Recent studies on the safety and efficacy of diluted doses of the smallpox vaccine, conducted primarily on young, healthy college student volunteers, resulted in a third of them missing work or school as a result of reactions to the vaccine. The result was confirmed by a CDC [Centers for Disease Control and Prevention] estimate cited in the GAO report.

Concern about the reaction is exacerbated by the fact that many hospitals will need to keep vaccinated employees away from vulnerable patients. The smallpox vaccine is a "live" vaccine that infects the recipient with a related virus. After being vaccinated, the recipient can spread this infection to others (called "contact vaccinia"). This is especially problematic in contemporary health care settings, where there are a large number of immunocompromised individuals—people who are HIV positive or are transplant recipients, for example. Some hospitals are considering furloughing vaccinated employees for up to three weeks to prevent the vaccinia virus from spreading to patients.

In late April 2003, Congress . . . passed the Smallpox Emergency Personnel Protection Act of 2003, which would reimburse those participating in smallpox response activities for injuries arising as a direct result of administration of the smallpox vaccine. The act will provide compensation for the "reasonable and necessary" costs of medical care associated with a vaccine-related injury and will pay up to $262,000 to the families of those who die as a result of the vaccine. Those suffering permanent disability can receive up to $50,000 a year annually through the compensation fund, and those who are temporarily or partially disabled can receive up to $262,000 in compensation for their injuries. However, the act leaves several significant questions about vaccination compensation unanswered: for example, which injuries will be eligible for reimbursement?

Deadly Complications

While agreement on the compensation issue is a step forward in implementing the administration's smallpox vaccination program, it is but one of a number of concerns inhibiting health worker participation in the vaccination program. Together, these concerns reflect a broad apprehension about the risks associated with the smallpox vaccine. Known risks include encephalitis (1 in 200,000 to 300,000), death (estimates range up to 3–5 per million), and other side effects that are serious enough to require a doctor's care (in sum, 1 of every 10,000 cases). Recently, three people have died of heart attacks after being vaccinated, several others have experienced heart problems, leading the CDC to issue new guidelines excluding those with heart conditions from the vaccination program. The renewed emphasis on risk has resulted in a general failure to gain sufficient volunteers for the health worker smallpox vaccination program. In the words of Representative Lois Capps (D-California), "Medical and public safety professionals know the risks of the disease and the vaccine very well, and few have been willing to take that risk . . . This initiative is failing."

The administration had hoped to vaccinate approximately 500,000 health workers within thirty days of the 24 January 2003 start date for the program. Ten weeks into it, less than 6 percent of the targeted number had been vaccinated, . . .

> *Medical and public safety professionals know the risks of the disease and the vaccine very well, and few have been willing to take that risk.*

Health care professionals' refusal to be vaccinated against smallpox presents a classic conflict between individual and public goods: how much risk should an individual health care professional be required to assume in order to attain a public good, in this case creating conditions for the timely distribution of smallpox vaccine, should an outbreak require mass vaccination of the general public? . . . [W]e will consider the ethical arguments for a professional obligation to subvert self-interest to the public good and argue that health care professionals have no such obligation, at least while bioterrorism employing smallpox is only a hypothetical and indeed very unlikely risk. . . .

Professional Obligations and Risk

One argument for a professional obligation to assume the risks of smallpox vaccination centers on a . . . general obligation for health care professionals to provide health care to patients in need despite some risk to their own health. The clearest analogy for this argument lies in the commonly recognized obligation of health care providers to treat patients with communicable diseases, such as TB [tuberculosis], yellow fever, polio, influenza. Discussions of this type of professional obligation were prominent in both the bioethics and popular literature in the early years of the HIV epidemic, when little was known about the nature of the infection or ways in which it might be spread. Both professional and public opinion condemned refusal to treat HIV-infected patients. The argument for an obligation to assume some degree of risk as a part of the health care profession is perhaps best illustrated by a statement issued by the Committee on Ethics of the American Nurses' Association concerning the professional responsibility to care for patients with infectious disease: "Nursing . . . creates a special relationship between nurse and patient, with special duties for the nurse. The nurse is not a 'stranger' and thus is not at liberty to walk away from those in need of nursing assistance."

But there are several problems with this way of establishing a professional obligation to be vaccinated against smallpox. First, the professional obligation to assume risk is normally centered around issues related to providing care in specific and extant cases involving the needs of a sick and vulnerable population. In contrast, pre-event vaccination involves preparing to treat abstract "possible cases." Further, the balance of harms in the case of treating patients with infectious diseases is significantly different from pre-event smallpox vaccination. Consider the mid-1980s literature on the professional obligation to treat HIV-infected individuals. That literature points to the serious harms to the patient that would result from a refusal to treat. . . .

> *❝ The smallpox vaccine is the most dangerous vaccine approved for large-scale use. ❞*

Pre-event smallpox vaccination, however, poses a significantly different balance of risks. The smallpox vaccine is the most dangerous vaccine approved for large-scale use. Its risks are exacerbated by the fact that the vaccine to be used under the Bush administration plan is either "old" vaccine that has been in storage for more than 30 years, or a "new" vaccine that is experimental (posing a special problem . . .). The risks of adverse reactions to smallpox vaccination, then, are not clearly less than the risks posed to the general public by a two- or three-day delay in vaccinating the general public after a terrorist attack that used smallpox, particularly given the unlikelihood that the attack would use smallpox. Smallpox is difficult to acquire, to handle, and to release effectively. Although these obstacles might be overcome, there are a number of other potential agents that pose fewer problems. Chemical agents are even easier to develop, and given the stockpiling of smallpox vaccine and development of plans to distribute the stockpile, a bioterror attack using smallpox would have limited effectiveness, and that fact makes it even less likely to be used.

George Annas [a bioethicist who studies ethical issues relating to medicine] has stated that physicians are not expected to be saints: if the patient's medical condition exposed the physician to great risk to life or health, she may be justified in refusing to provide treatment even in emergency situations. . . .

Beyond the risks to individual health care providers, there are significant concerns about the effects of smallpox vaccination for health care workers on an already strained health care system. First, there will be a need to replace health workers who become sick from adverse reactions to the vaccine. This will be costly in the context of a current nursing shortage in which many hospitals are already understaffed. This is in addition to the staffing costs in terms of public health personnel, and the costs associated with personnel having to receive, administer, and follow-up on vaccinations, including time for planning, education, training, screening, data management, and treatment of adverse events. In this context, Patrick Lenihan, deputy commissioner of the Chicago Public Health Department, has stated: "It's been disruptive. . . . People who were doing routine health activities six months ago like taking blood pressures and assessing diabetes are now spending time preparing for smallpox vaccination and treatment."

> **❝** There will be a need to replace health workers who become sick from adverse reactions to the vaccine. **❞**

In addition, concerns have been expressed by health care professionals that adverse reactions to the smallpox vaccine could result in loss of public confidence in other, much safer vaccines, such as the [measles-mumps-rubella and diptheria-pertussis-tetanus] vaccines routinely given to children, or the flu vaccine that is important to people with compromised immune systems and the elderly. Such a loss in confidence could have a significant impact on public health, as the success of vaccination programs is dependent on continued high rates of vaccination in order to maintain "herd immunity." Since no vaccine is 100 percent effective, loss of herd immunity poses risk both to those who refuse vaccination, as well as some percentage of those who are vaccinated. . . .

Professional Obligations and National Security

Another argument for the obligation of health care professionals to be vaccinated against smallpox is that health care professionals represent the "front lines" of national defense against biological terrorism. Thus, health care professionals have a national security obligation, as "front line soldiers in the war on terror," to assume the risks associated with vaccination similar to that of military personnel. The National Intelligence Council of the Central Intelligence Agency, for example, has characterized bioterrorism as not only an issue for public health, but also as a national security concern.

Establishing a professional obligation on the basis of national security interests, however, requires that we establish a public responsibility for health care professionals beyond that of ordinary citizens. Arguments for this type of responsibility have been advanced in other contexts. For example, some arguments for an ethical obligation to treat HIV patients centered around the idea that as members of a healing profession, physicians are obligated to subordinate self-interest to a duty of altruism. Others have argued that as professionals, doctors and nurses have ethical obligations beyond their duties as citizens. . . .

This approach, too, however, is fraught with problems. We can understand the basis of obligation for professional military personnel, for example, to assume risks in order to protect national security in this way. Protection against smallpox might be deemed necessary for military personnel in order to avoid a loss of military capability. There are several historical examples of a contagious disease spreading among the troops and significantly reducing military capacity. Since entrance into the military profession involves the explicit recognition that one's own welfare (and even life) will be subverted to the interests of national security, the fact that a refusal to be vaccinated might threaten military capacity provides a plausible grounds for a professional obligation to be vaccinated among the military.

Health care professionals do not obviously have the same

type of national security duties as the result of their member-
ship in a health profession, however. While it is true that health
care professionals possess skills unique to their profession that
are vital for the treatment and containment of (natural or
terror-related) epidemics, possession of these skills does not nec-
essarily require that they assume risks beyond those required of
ordinary citizens in order to protect national security. A person
enters the health profession and acquires those skills in order to
pursue quite different goals: treating the sick. . . . There is a significant difference between the obligation to assume risk in this
context and the obligation to be vaccinated against smallpox
pre-event. At most, one might argue that a collective obligation
exists for the profession as a whole to assume risks to secure the
public welfare. But this broad obligation could not easily be
translated to a professional obligation for any particular individual. As we have discussed earlier, the CDC's estimate of the
delay that incomplete pre-event vaccination would cause in
vaccinating the general public is minimal (even if that estimate
is optimistic and the delay were slightly longer). Given this relatively short delay, along with the remote chance of an actual
bioterror attack using smallpox, the delay does not seem to represent a significant threat to national security.

11

The Use of Nonlethal Chemical Weapons Should Be Prohibited

Mark Wheelis

Mark Wheelis is a microbiologist at the University of California–Davis, and a member of the Working Group on Chemical and Biological Weapons Control of the Federation of American Scientists.

Chemical weapons of certain types can be employed with deadly efficiency. However, there is another class of chemical weapons that receives much less attention. Called "nonlethal" weapons, they are meant to incapacitate, rather than kill. Sometimes used by law enforcement personnel in hostage situations, these weapons are misnamed. Nonlethal chemical weapons can kill up to 20 percent of their victims. Yet the United States would like to use them in Iraq and for other military purposes. If this were to happen, the United States would be in violation the 1993 Chemical Weapons Convention that is almost universally interpreted as banning their use. President George W. Bush should condemn the military use of nonlethal weapons and urge other nations to do the same. Chemical incapacitants can be deadly and are little different from the biological weapons denounced by the U.S. government. These agents should remain off-limits for use in war.

On October 26, 2002, approximately 50 Chechen separatist guerrillas took over a Moscow theater, holding about 750

Mark Wheelis, "Nonlethal Chemical Weapons," *Issues in Science and Technology*, vol. 19, Spring 2003. Copyright © 2003 by the University of Texas at Dallas, Richardson, TX. Reproduced by permission.

people hostage. The hostage-takers were well armed with automatic weapons and grenades, and the females were wired with high explosives. They demanded the withdrawal of Russian troops from [the breakaway republic of] Chechnya, and threatened to kill the hostages and themselves if their demand was not met. The Russian government refused to negotiate. On the 28th, Russian special forces troops stormed the theater, first releasing a potent narcotic (a derivative of the opiate anesthetic fentanyl) into the ventilation system. When the troops burst into the main hall, they found the hostages and hostage-takers in a coma. The unconscious Chechens were all shot dead at point blank range, and the hostages were rushed to hospitals. In the end, approximately 125 hostages died of overdose; the rest—more than 600—survived. A number of the survivors are likely to have permanent disability. Opiate overdose causes respiratory depression that can starve the brain of oxygen, causing permanent brain damage when prolonged. It took hours to evacuate and treat the hostages. Aspiration pneumonia, a frequent complication of opiate overdose, may also cause permanent damage.

> *Used by terrorists in conjunction with other weapons, such as incendiary devices or high explosives, chemical incapacitants could prevent flight and thus increase death tolls.*

This dramatic event brought into focus a debate that has been simmering in arms control circles for several years, barely noticed by the general public: whether "nonlethal" chemical weapons are legal, and, if they are, whether it is a good idea to develop them. Proponents have argued for some time that situations exactly like the one in Moscow justify the use of such weapons. A more likely result, however, is that these weapons will turn out to be a Faustian bargain—[an agreement characterized by] temporary benefits and high costs.

Was the chemical attack during the Moscow hostage rescue legal under international law? The 1993 Chemical Weapons Convention (CWC) bans the development, production, stockpiling, and use of chemical weapons. It defines chemical weapons as all toxic chemicals and all devices specifically designed to deliver them. Toxic chemicals are defined as chemicals that "cause death, temporary incapacitation, or permanent harm to humans or animals." Thus, chemical incapacitants are clearly prohibited. (The term chemical incapacitant is preferable to nonlethal chemical weapon because none of the possible agents is really nonlethal, as the death of so many Moscow hostages dramatically demonstrated.)

Under the CWC, however, there are four specific purposes for which toxic chemicals can be used without being considered chemical weapons: peaceful medical, agricultural, research, or pharmaceutical purposes; protective purposes (such as testing defenses against chemical weapons); military purposes not dependent on toxicity (many compounds in high explosives and other munitions are toxic, but their toxicity is irrelevant to their function); and "law enforcement including domestic riot control." The first three of these are not relevant here, but the fourth clearly is. In Moscow, Russia was enforcing its own domestic law on its own territory, and so the use of a chemical incapacitant did not violate the CWC. Whether the development, production, and stockpiling of the agent was originally intended for this purpose, and therefore legal, is unknown.

Thus there are two rather different questions: Given that it is legal to develop and use these weapons for law enforcement purposes, is it wise? And how should prohibited military development be deterred?

Little Utility for Law Enforcement

Any program developing chemical incapacitants has to start with the realization that they are dangerous and will cause a significant death toll when used at levels that will incapacitate most of those exposed. How high a toll is hard to estimate with certainty, but even with optimistic assumptions, lethality of 10–20 percent has to be expected, which is what happened in Moscow. Therefore they should be used only as a last resort.

But could it work twice? The Moscow hostage rescue could be considered a success, since more than 80 percent of the hostages were recovered alive. But the next time terrorists engage in hostage-taking, they will certainly be prepared for the use of incapacitants, with gas masks and possibly antidotes. (There is a readily available and effective antagonist to opiates.) Such minimal preparations will completely defeat the advantage of chemical incapacitants and render them nearly useless for the specific scenario that proponents cite as requiring them.

Since we can assume that terrorists or criminals would be prepared to defend themselves against chemical incapacitants, what legitimate uses would there be for such desperate measures? I believe that they have little utility for law enforcement in democratic societies.

But criminals, terrorists, and dictators will find them to be quite useful. The ideal targets for chemical incapacitants are people who cannot protect themselves, perhaps do not even expect an attack, and whose death is acceptable. Used by terrorists in conjunction with other weapons, such as incendiary devices or high explosives, chemical incapacitants could prevent flight and thus increase death tolls. Or they could provide a means to neutralize security forces silently, preserving surprise in the first few minutes of an attack on targets such as government buildings. Criminals might also find uses for such weapons; there is already a serious problem with chemical incapacitants being used to facilitate rape. Security forces in despotic regimes could use these agents to immobilize protesters rather than disperse them, as is done with existing riot control agents, thus allowing protesters to be taken into state custody. If chemical incapacitants become weapons in the arsenal of law enforcement agencies, they will enter the legal global trade in police weapons and be as available to despotic regimes as they are to democracies. They will also quickly enter the black market in arms, where they will be readily available to criminals and terrorists.

> *There is no basis whatsoever for calling [chemical incapacitants] nonlethal or less lethal or any of the other euphemisms that proponents use to imply a categorical difference.*

Like all chemical weapons, chemical incapacitants are primarily weapons for attacking the defenseless. Chemical weapons were used extensively in World War I, but neither side gained any significant advantage from them, because both sides were able to develop them and both deployed defenses. But after the war, several countries used them effectively against tribal peoples unable to defend themselves or retaliate in kind: the Spanish in Morocco, the British in Afghanistan, and the Italians in Ethiopia. Chemical incapacitants will be the same: relatively ineffectual weapons for law enforcement because of their significant lethality and the ease of defense. But in the hands of terrorists, criminals, torturers, or despots, who care little about the lethality and whose victims are defenseless, they could pose a serious threat.

Military Use of Incapacitants

Of course, militaries would have additional uses for such weapons if they were willing to ignore the legal obstacles. Chemical incapacitants could have utility in urban warfare and in military operations other than war (counterterrorism, peacekeeping, and so forth). They would be quite attractive to special forces, which could use them to silently incapacitate opponents behind enemy lines. Thus stockpiles of chemical incapacitants for law enforcement would pose a nearly irresistible temptation to those who wanted to divert them to military purposes.

Would this be a bad thing? Nonlethal weapons are often perceived as a humane alternative to lethal weapons. Yet chemical incapacitants cause levels of lethality comparable to those of military firearms (about 35 percent), artillery (about 20 percent), grenades (about 10 percent), and civilian handguns (about 10 percent). Chemical weapons used in World War I were similar; they killed about 7 percent of casualties. Chemical incapacitants are clearly in the same category with respect to their lethality: There is no basis whatsoever for calling [chemical incapacitants] nonlethal or less lethal or any of the other euphemisms that proponents use to imply a categorical difference.

Furthermore, the military use of nonlethal weapons is more often an adjunct to, not a replacement for, lethal force. The history of the U.S. military use of tear gas is a case in point. During the Vietnam War, the United States used tear gas extensively. The public rationale was identical to that now being cited for chemical incapacitants: humanitarian goals of reducing civilian deaths in situations in which combatants and noncombatants were mixed. Although tear gas was occasionally used for that purpose, the major use by far was to drive enemy troops from cover and make them more vulnerable to small arms fire, artillery, and aerial bombing. Thousands of tons of tear gas were used between 1966 and 1969, disseminated in hand grenades, rifle-propelled grenades, artillery shells, rockets, bombs, and helicopter-mounted bulk dispensers. Although considered highly successful by the military, the practice was widely condemned, and in 1975 President Ford issued Executive Order (EO) 11850, which restricted the use of riot control agents to "defensive military modes to save lives," such as riot control in territories under U.S. control, cases where civilians are used as shields, the rescue of downed aircrews or escaping prisoners-of-war, and use behind the lines to protect convoys.

The United States, alone among the 150 parties to the CWC, argues that the convention allows riot control agents. The argument rests in part on the CWC's different definitions of toxic chemicals (causing "death, temporary incapacitation, or permanent harm to humans or animals") versus riot control agents (chemicals that "can produce rapidly in humans sensory irritation or disabling physical effects which disappear within a short time following termination of exposure"). Thus, the United States does not consider "sensory irritation or disabling physical effects" to be a form of "temporary incapacitation." It also does not consider these chemicals to be toxic, despite the fact that they have caused many deaths and permanent disability.

> **"** Rear Admiral Stephen Baker has claimed that special forces are now equipped with 'knockout gases' that he [expected would] be used in Iraq if needed. **"**

The United States thus asserts that military use of riot control agents is limited by the CWC only by a single sentence: "Riot control agents may not be used "as a method of warfare." This prohibition would prevent future use of riot control agents in the way they were used in Vietnam, but the United States believes that it permits their use under the terms of EO 11850. Indeed, Secretary of Defense Donald Rumsfeld testified to Congress [in 2003] that he intended to request presidential approval to use riot control agents in case of war with Iraq. This would be most unfortunate, because the rest of the world would consider this to be chemical warfare. It would vitiate the U.S. argument that the war is a moral one, with part of its purpose being to enforce the CWC.

Despite its uniquely liberal interpretation of the CWC restrictions on the use of riot control agents, it is hard to imagine that even the United States could consider chemical incapacitants as anything other than toxic chemicals, and thus fully covered by the CWC. The intent of chemical incapacitants is, after all, to temporarily incapacitate victims, and their high lethality (compared with riot control agents) makes it clear that they are toxic chemicals. Thus the development of such agents as weapons would, in order to be legal, have to be for law enforcement purposes only; no military development, production, possession, or use would be permitted.

> *The pursuit of chemical incapacitants is likely to be the first step in the exploitation of pharmacology and biotechnology for hostile purposes.*

What might such a legal program look like? It would be administered, performed, and funded by nonmilitary agencies, such as the Department of Justice. The rationale under which approval is secured would mention only law enforcement purposes. The work would be unclassified. The safety requirement for agents would be compatible with domestic use. The munitions developed to deliver the agent would be those in common use by police.

Unfortunately, U.S. research into chemical incapacitants fails to satisfy these criteria. Most of the projects have been originated and funded by the military. The rationales refer almost exclusively to military scenarios, including urban warfare, military operations other than war, and even major theater war. Much of the work is classified. And a 81-mm mortar shell with a range of several miles is being developed to deliver "nonlethal" payloads, including chemicals. Only in the area of safety standards does the U.S. program appear to be consistent with law enforcement; the goal is an agent that causes less than 0.5 percent fatalities (comparable to tear gas).

Although research per se is not prohibited by the CWC, and it appears (at least on the basis of unclassified material) that the United States has not yet passed the threshold of prohibited chemical weapons development, its research is nevertheless provocative and destabilizing. The overt interest in prohibited agents and the repeated assertion that they could have military utility make it appear that it is only the lack so far of a suitable agent that has prevented the United States from entering prohibited territory. This perception, whether accurate or not, seriously erodes the U.S. claim to the moral high ground vis-à-vis countries like Iraq.

Of course, much of the U.S. research on chemical incapacitants may be classified, and this further reduces the confidence others can have in U.S. compliance with the CWC. Although the lead agency in this effort (the Marine Corps' Joint Non-Lethal Weapons Directorate) has denied any current efforts to develop chemical incapacitants, retired Rear Admiral Stephen Baker has claimed that special forces are now equipped with "knockout gases" that he [expected would] be used in Iraq if needed. Clarification of this serious charge is urgently needed.

It would do a great deal of good if President Bush or Secretary Rumsfeld would unambiguously disavow any intent to develop chemical incapacitants as military weapons, deny any current possession or deployment (or, if necessary, order their immediate destruction), and explicitly acknowledge that such incapacitants are prohibited by the CWC. If this were coupled to a commitment to forgo the use of riot control agents against Iraq, the United States could recapture some of the legitimacy lost because of ambiguity concerning its own compliance with the CWC.

The Potential for Misuse

The pursuit of chemical incapacitants for law enforcement purposes will turn out to be a Faustian bargain at best; their pursuit for military purposes would violate the CWC. By far the best policy option is to eschew this category of weapon entirely and to exert leadership in the international arena to ensure that others do the same.

Although there is some possibility that chemical incapacitants might be useful law enforcement tools in certain special circumstances, the ease of protection against them means that such circumstances will be rare. Their utility will thus be very limited and not worth the price that inevitably would have to be paid.

The price is high in many ways. Incapacitants have a much greater potential to be used by dictators, terrorists, or criminals than by law enforcement. And the temptation to divert such weapons to military uses will be immense. Certainly the world has taken note of the persistent U.S. military interest and the apparent Russian stockpiles. Many nations probably disbelieve U.S. claims that it is restricting itself to permitted research activities, and may thus be encouraged to begin their own clandestine development and stockpiling. In this way a new chemical arms race may begin.

Even if development and stockpiling of incapacitants were scrupulously restricted to law enforcement purposes, the CWC would nonetheless be fundamentally undermined. The overarching purpose of the CWC is to prevent nations from entering military conflict with chemical weapons that they are prohibited from using. The ban on use is secondary, since that ban has been in place since the 1920s. If we permit stockpiles of chemical incapacitants for law enforcement that could be instantly redirected to military use, we have seriously subverted the CWC.

In the long run, the pursuit of chemical incapacitants is likely to be the first step in the exploitation of pharmacology and biotechnology for hostile purposes. It would be naive to think that this exploitation could be confined to domestic law enforcement. Even if the more trustworthy nations observe their treaty commitments, many others will be seduced by the military utility of pharmacological weapons. And during the next several decades, scientific advances will almost certainly see a tremendous expansion of our capabilities to manipulate human consciousness, emotions, motor control, reproductive capacity, behavior, and so forth. Such capacities have potential for great medical benefits, and this potential (along with the profits that could be made in applying the benefits) ensures that progress will be rapid. But they also have entirely novel and terrifying potential for abuse. Our challenge is to bequeath to our children a future in which the benefits of biotechnology and pharmacology are realized, but their abuses contained. This is a formidable challenge; no militarily useful technology has ever been successfully eschewed.

One important measure would be a new international treaty that prohibits the hostile manipulation of human physiology, particularly with respect to the central nervous system and reproductive physiology. The European Parliament has already called for "a global ban on all developments and deployments of weapons which might enable any form of manipulation of human beings," and the International Committee of the Red Cross has urged states "to adopt at a high political level an international Declaration on Biotechnology, Weapons and Humanity containing a renewed commitment to existing norms and specific commitments to future preventative action." Given the rapid rate of scientific progress, it is urgent to establish a clear understanding that any manipulation of human biochemistry or genetics for hostile purposes is completely unacceptable. A new international convention would be an important step in establishing such a norm.

Negotiating a new international treaty will take years. More immediately, Congress should initiate active oversight of the nonlethal weapons programs of the Departments of Defense, Energy, and Justice, of the Central Intelligence Agency, and of any other agencies involved. Such oversight should pay specific attention to the long-term policy issues. Since much of this research is probably classified, and thus unknowable to the media or the public, only congressional oversight can ensure that it is conducted in accordance with the best long-term interests of the United States and the world. The long-term potential of biotechnology and pharmacology to be used to do harm is too serious a policy issue to be left to the military, where short-term tactical considerations may lead to unwise decisions.

The United States is certain to be the critical player; it is the world's preeminent biotechnology and pharmaceutical power, and the world's foremost military power. For better or worse, the United States will lead the way into the exploitation of biotechnology as weaponry or into a robust ethical and political system preventing such exploitation. The choice is ours; we should make it actively, and not slide unwittingly into a future we have not chosen and may bitterly regret.

Organizations to Contact

The editors have compiled the following list of organizations concerned with the issues debated in this book. The descriptions are derived from materials provided by the organizations. All have publications or information available for interested readers. The list was compiled on the date of publication of the present volume; names, addresses, phone and fax numbers, and e-mail addresses may change. Be aware that many organizations take several weeks or longer to respond to inquiries, so allow as much time as possible.

Biohazard News
925 Lakeville St., PO Box 251, Petaluma, CA 94952
e-mail: info@biohazardnews.net
Web site: www.biohazardnews.net/index.htm

Biohazard News is a volunteer-run organization dedicated to providing the public timely information about the threat of biological terrorism, which it believes to be one of the most serious threats to America's national security. It publishes a free newsletter and maintains a Web site that includes interviews and information on biological weapons and terrorist groups.

Carnegie Endowment for International Peace
1779 Massachusetts Ave. NW, Washington, DC 20036
(202) 483-7600 • fax: (202) 483-1840
e-mail: info@ceip.org • Web site: www.ceip.org

The Carnegie Endowment for International Peace conducts research on international affairs and U.S. foreign policy. Issues concerning nuclear weapons and proliferation are often discussed in articles published in its quarterly journal *Foreign Policy*.

Center for Biosecurity of UPMC
Pier IV Bldg., 621 E. Pratt St., Suite 210, Baltimore, MD 21202
(443) 573-3304 • fax: (443) 573-3305
Web site: www.upmc-biosecurity.org

The Center for Biosecurity is an independent, nonprofit organization of the University of Pittsburgh Medical Center (UPMC). The Center for Biosecurity works to prevent the development and use of biological weapons, to study advances in science and governance that diminish the power of biological weapons as agents of mass lethality, and to develop measures to lessen the illness, death, and civil disruption that would result if prevention efforts fail. The organization publishes the *Biosecurity Journal* and the online *Biosecurity Bulletin* newsletter.

Center for Nonproliferation Studies
Monterey Institute of International Studies
460 Pierce St., Monterey, CA 93940
(831) 647-4154 • fax: (831) 647-3519
e-mail: cns@miis.edu • Web site: http://cns.miis.edu

The Center for Nonproliferation Studies researches all aspects of nonproliferation and works to combat the spread of biological weapons and other weapons of mass destruction. The center provides research databases and has multiple reports, papers, speeches, and congressional testimony online. The *Nonproliferation Review*, its main publication, is published quarterly.

Center for Strategic and International Studies
1800 K St. NW, Suite 400, Washington, DC 20006
(202) 887-0200 • fax: (202) 775-3199
e-mail: webmaster@csis.org • Web site: www.csis.org

The Center for Strategic and International Studies works to provide world leaders with strategic insights and policy options on current and emerging global issues. It publishes books, including *Combating Chemical, Biological, Radiological, and Nuclear Terrorism*. The *Washington Quarterly*, a journal on political, economic, and security issues, and other publications including reports can be downloaded from its Web site.

Centers for Disease Control and Prevention (CDC)
1600 Clifton Rd., Atlanta, GA 30333
(800) 311-3435
e-mail: netinfo@cdc.gov • Web site: www.cdc.gov

The Centers for Disease Control and Prevention is a government agency charged with protecting the public health of the nation by preventing and controlling diseases and by responding to public health emergencies. Programs of the CDC include the National Center for Infectious Diseases, which publishes the journal *Emerging Infectious Diseases*. Information on potential biological warfare agents, including anthrax and smallpox, is available on the CDC Web site.

Chemical and Biological Arms Control Institute
1747 Pennsylvania Ave. NW, 7th Fl., Washington, DC 20006
(202) 296-3550 • fax: (202) 296-3574
e-mail: cbaci@cbaci.org • Web site: www.cbaci.org/cbaci/index.html

The institute is a nonprofit corporation that supports arms control and nonproliferation, particularly of biological and chemical weapons. In addition to conducting research, the institute plans meetings and seminars and assists in the implementation of weapons control treaties. Its publications include the *Dispatch*, published bimonthly, and numerous fact sheets, monographs, and reports.

Henry L. Stimson Center
11 Dupont Circle NW, 9th Fl., Washington, DC 20036
(202) 223-5956 • fax: (202) 238-9604
e-mail: info@stimson.org • Web site: www.stimson.org

The Henry L. Stimson Center is an independent public policy institute committed to finding and promoting innovative solutions to the security challenges confronting the United States and other nations. The center directs the Chemical and Biological Weapons Nonproliferation Project, which serves as a clearinghouse of information related to the monitoring and implementation of the 1972 Biological Weapons Convention. The center produces reports, papers, and books on policy on biological and other weapons of mass destruction.

Heritage Foundation
214 Massachusetts Ave. NE, Washington, DC 20002
(202) 546-4400 • (800) 544-4843 • fax: (202) 544-2260
e-mail: pubs@heritage.org • Web site: www.heritage.org

The Heritage Foundation is a conservative public policy research institute that supports the principles of free enterprise and limited government in environmental matters. Its many publications include the monthly *Policy Review* and position papers concerning terrorism, privacy rights, and constitutional issues.

Sunshine Project
101 W. Sixth St., Suite 607, Austin, TX 78701
(512) 494-0545
e-mail: tsp@sunshine-project.org • Web site: www.sunshine-project.org

The Sunshine Project is an international nongovernmental organization that works to avert the dangers of new weapons stemming from advances in biotechnology. It conducts research and issues reports on biological-weapons research in Germany, the United States, and other countries. These reports and other information on biological weapons can be downloaded from its Web site.

U.S. Arms Control and Disarmament Agency (ACDA)
320 Twenty-first St. NW, Washington, DC 20451
(800) 581-ACDA • fax: (202) 647-6928
Web site: www.acda.gov

The mission of the U.S. Arms Control and Disarmament Agency is to strengthen the national security of the United States by formulating, advocating, negotiating, implementing, and verifying effective arms control, nonproliferation, and disarmament policies, strategies, and agreements. In so doing, ACDA ensures that arms control is fully integrated into the development and conduct of U.S. national security policy. The agency publishes fact sheets on the disarmament of weapons of mass destruction as well as online records of speeches, treaties, and reports related to arms control.

U.S. Department of State, Bureau of Nonproliferation
Public Communications Division
2201 C St. NW, Washington, DC 20520
(202) 647-6575
Web site: www.state.gov/t/np

102

The Bureau of Nonproliferation leads U.S. efforts to prevent the spread of weapons of mass destruction, including biological weapons. The bureau has primary responsibility for leadership in the interagency process for nonproliferation issues, leads major nonproliferation negotiations and discussions with other countries, and participates in all nonproliferation-related dialogues. Its Web site offers speeches and news briefings on U.S. foreign policy related to biological weapons.

Bibliography

Books

Angelo Acquista   *The Survival Guide: What to Do in a Biological, Chemical, or Nuclear Emergency.* New York: Random House Trade Paperbacks, 2003.

Yonah Alexander and Milton Hoenig, eds.   *Super Terrorism: Biological, Chemical, and Nuclear.* Ardsley, NY: Transnational, 2001.

Wendy Barnaby   *The Plague Makers: The Secret World of Biological Warfare.* New York: Continuum, 2000.

Jim A. Davis and Barry R. Schneider, eds.   *The Gathering Biological Warfare Storm.* Maxwell Air Force Base, AL: USAF Counterproliferation Center, 2002.

Anthony S. Fauci   *Bioterrorism: A Clear and Present Danger.* Santa Monica, CA: RAND, 2003.

William H. Frist   *When Every Moment Counts: What You Need to Know About Bioterrorism from the Senate's Only Doctor.* Lanham, MD: Rowman & Littlefield, 2002.

Steve Goodwin   *Biological Terrorism.* San Francisco: Benjamin Cummings, 2003.

Jeanne Guillemin   *Biological Weapons: From the Invention of State-Sponsored Programs to Contemporary Bioterrorism.* New York: Columbia University Press, 2004.

Theodore William Karasik   *Toxic Warfare.* Santa Monica, CA: RAND, 2002.

Peter R. Lavoy, Scott D. Sagan, and James J. Wirtz   *Planning the Unthinkable: How New Powers Will Use Nuclear, Biological, and Chemical Weapons.* Ithaca, NY: Cornell University Press, 2000.

Herbert M. Levine   *Chemical & Biological Weapons in Our Times.* New York: Franklin Watts, 2000.

Albert J. Mauroni   *Chemical and Biological Warfare: A Reference Handbook.* Santa Barbara, CA: ABC-CLIO, 2003.

Judith Miller   *Germs: Biological Weapons and America's Secret War.* New York: Simon & Schuster, 2001.

Mike T. Osterholm and John Schwartz   *Living Terrors: What America Needs to Know to Survive the Coming Bioterrorist Catastrophe.* New York: H.W. Wilson, 1999.

Simon M. Whitby   *Biological Warfare Against Crops.* New York: Palgrave, 2002.

103

104

Susan Wright, ed.   *Biological Warfare and Disarmament: New Problems/New Perspectives.* Lanham, MD: Rowan & Littlefield, 2002.

Periodicals

Ted Agres   "Companies on the Fence About Biodefense: What Will It Take to Make Vaccines and Drugs for Smallpox, Ebola, and Plague Look Like Enticing Business Prospects?" *Scientist*, October 25, 2004.

Dlawer Ala'Aldeen   "Risk of Deliberately Induced Anthrax Outbreak," *Lancet*, October 27, 2001.

Kerry Boyd   "U.S. Grapples with Use of Nonlethal Agents," *Arms Control Today*, April 2003.

Jeffrey Brent   "Toxic Terror: Assessing Terrorist Use of Chemical and Biological Weapons," *Journal of Toxicology: Clinical Toxicology*, October 2003.

Kathryn Brown   "Up in the Air: The Government Is Pouring Money into Sensors to Detect Bioweapons, but Skeptics Question Whether They Can Really Protect the Public from the Array of Potential Threats," *Science*, August 27, 2004.

Hillel W. Cohen, Robert M. Gould, and Victor W. Sidel   "The Pitfalls of Bioterrorism Preparedness: The Anthrax and Smallpox Experiences," *American Journal of Public Health*, October 2004.

Harry W. Conley   "Not with Impunity: Assessing US Policy for Retaliating to a Chemical or Biological Attack," *Air & Space Power Journal*, Spring 2003.

Lorenzo Cortes   "Industry's Confidence High on Biological Detection Technologies," *Defense Daily*, November 19, 2004.

Nicole Deller and John Burroughs   "Arms Control Abandoned: The Case of Biological Weapons," *World Policy Journal*, Summer 2003.

Martin Enserinik   "On Biowarfare's Frontline: Heightened Fears of Bioterrorism Have Shone the Spotlight on the Army's Biodefense Lab—and Pulled Its Researchers Out of Their Isolation," *Science*, June 14, 2002.

Demetrius Evison, David Hinsley, and Paul Rice   "Chemical Weapons," *British Medical Journal*, February 9, 2002.

Sydney J. Freedberg Jr. and Marilyn Werber Serafini   "Be Afraid, Be Moderately Afraid," *National Journal*, March 27, 1999.

Peter Huber   "The Biosniffers Are Coming," *Forbes*, June 23, 2004.

Marylia Kelley and Jay Coghlan	"Mixing Bugs and Bombs: Siting Advanced Bioweapons Germ Research at Secretive Nuclear Labs Could Be a Serious Mistake, Especially Given Energy's Poor Security, Safety, and Environmental Records," *Bulletin of the Atomic Scientists*, September/October 2003.
Michael T. Klare	"Nonproliferation Politics," *Nation*, October 11, 2004.
Milton Leitenberg	"Biological Weapons and Bioterrorism in the First Years of the Twenty-first Century," *Politics and the Life Sciences*, September 2002.
Alex John London	"Threats to the Common Good: Biochemical Weapons and Human Subjects Research," *Hastings Center Report*, September/October 2003.
David Malakoff	"Security Rules Leave Labs Wanting More Guidance: Scientists Criticize Flaws in the U.S. Government's Plan to Oversee Research on Material That Could Be Used as Bioweapons," *Science*, February 21, 2003.
Mac Margolis	"A Mix-Up in Priorities: By Lavishing Money on Cures for Bioterror Attack, America Ignores Prosaic Diseases That Kill Millions," *Newsweek International*, April 5, 2004.
Thomas May	"Political Authority in a Bioterror Emergency," *Journal of Law, Medicine & Ethics*, Spring 2004.
Michael McCarthy	"USA Moves Quickly to Push Biodefence Research," *Lancet*, September 7, 2002.
Judith Miller	"When Is a Bomb Not a Bomb? Germ Experts Confront U.S.," *New York Times*, September 5, 2001.
James Randerson	"US in Danger of Breaking Chemical Weapons Treaty," *New Scientist*, April 5, 2003.
Diana Jean Schemo	"After 9/11, Universities Are Destroying Biological Agents," *New York Times*, December 17, 2002.
Chana R. Schoenberger and Emily Lambert	"Missing in Action: Many Thousands of Nuclear, Chemical and Biological Weapons Scientists Are Scattered Throughout the World, Working for Various Governments," *Forbes*, March 31, 2003.
William G. Schulz	"Science at a Time of Terror," *Chemical & Engineering News*, January 27, 2003.
Sharon Weinberger	"Pentagon Official Pushes for Higher Chem-Bio Defense Spending," *Defense Daily*, December 22, 2003.

Index

ABC news, 7
Acquista, Angelo, 29
Advisory Committee on
    Immunization Practices (ACIP), 76
Afghanistan, 12, 92
agroterrorism, 17–18, 62, 64, 67
Alfred P. Murrah Federal Building, 15
Alibek, Ken, 37, 38
American Academy of Family
    Physicians, 82
American Academy of Pediatricians,
    82
American Chemistry Council (ACC),
    32–34
American Medical Association, 74, 82
American Nurses' Association, 85
Annan, Kofi, 7
Annas, George, 86
anthrax
    attacks, 7, 8–9
        risk of, 24
        scenario for, 20
        during World War I, 12
    genetic engineering of , by Russia,
        57
    incubation period for, 15–16
    in Kazakhstan, 36, 37–38
    terrorists and, 52
asphyxiating agents, 7–8
Atlas, Ron, 45
Atshabar, Bakyt, 35–36
attacks
    actual risk of harm is minimal,
        23–26
    biological
        analysis of agents used in, 44
        prevention of, 65–67
        Q fever, 16
        responses to, 63–64, 67–70
        scenarios for, 17–20
        smallpox, 73–74
    chemical, 8, 25, 28, 29
        ricin, 52
        tear gas, 93–94
    on food supply, 17–18, 62, 64, 67
    1993 World Trade Center, 14–15,
        29–30
    psychological effects of potential,
        22–23
    reasons for, 16–17
    September 11, 2001, 11–12, 15

    see also anthrax, attacks
Aulisio, Mark P., 81
Aum Shinrikyo cult, 13, 14
"axis of evil," 37

Bacillus anthracis. See anthrax
Bailey, Pat, 46, 47–48
Baker, Stephen, 96
Bhagwan Shree Rajneesh cult, 13, 14
Bhopal (India), 30
bin Laden, Osama, 36–37
biodefense
    elements of, 62–65, 69
    funding for, 51
    national security requires
        development of, 21
    prevention of attacks and, 65–67
    research and
        facilities for
            opposition to location of,
                41–43, 46–49
            safety of, 42, 43–44, 45, 46–47,
                55–56
            secrecy about, 45
            suspicions of other nations
                provoked by, 54–55
        measures to build international
            confidence and, 56–59
    threat assessment for, 52–59,
        65–66, 67
Biodefense for the 21st Century,
    63–70
Biological Weapons Convention
    (BWC), 51, 52–53, 56, 58
Biosafety Levels, 43–44, 46
Biothreat Characterization Center,
    53–54
BioWatch program, 62
bioweapons
    are serious threat, 12–17, 61–62
    con, 23–26, 39
    construction of, 9
    ease of use of, 13–14, 85–86
    in former Soviet Union, 35–36,
        37–39
    incubation period for, 15–16
    moral restraints will not prevent
        use of, 14–15
    used during wars, 12–13, 24–25
    see also specific agents
Boca Raton, Florida, 7

Boston University Medicine Center (BUMC), 42, 48–49
Boyd, Susan, 46, 48
bubonic plague, 24–25
Bush, George W., 60
  biodefense plans of, 41, 43, 51, 63–70
    arms race could be provoked by, 54–56
    basis of, is flawed, 52–53
    response of, to possible attacks, 26
    smallpox vaccination plans of, 82
  on terrorists obtaining WMDs, 37
  on threat of bioweapons, 9
  on WMDs in Iraq, 28

California, University of
  at Davis, 41–42, 45–48
Canada, 57
Capps, Lois, 84
Carus, Seth, 13, 14
casualties, care of, 68
CBS news, 7
Centers for Disease Control and Prevention (CDC), 73, 75–76, 77
Chechen separatists, 89–90, 91
Chemical Facilities Security Act (2003), 33
chemical weapons
  are serious threat, 28
    con, 29–30
  attacks on plants with, are serious threat, 30, 31–34
  nonlethal, 89–91
    should be prohibited, 91–92, 95–98
  types of, 7–8, 25, 52, 93–94
  used in wars, 92–94, 95, 96, 97
  see also specific agents
Chemical Weapons Convention (CWC)
  provisions of, 90–91, 94
  purpose of, 97
  research and, 95
  U.S. compliance with, 96
China, 24–25
chlorine, effect of, 7
Cipro, 8
Clinton, Hillary, 42
Conant, Eve, 35
Cordesman, Anthony, 29
cyanide gas, 29–30
cyanide salts, 8

Daschle, Tom, 7
Davis, Jim A., 10
Divis, Dee Ann, 40
"dual-use" research, 58

Dugway Proving Ground (Utah), 43

environment, 29, 42–43
Ethiopia, 92–93
European Union, 57
Executive Order (EO) 11850, 94

Fink, Gerald R., 58
first responders, smallpox vaccination of, 72, 74, 77–78
food supply, attacks on, 17–18, 62, 64, 67
Ford, Gerald, 94

genetic engineering
  of anthrax by Russia, 57
  of pathogens, 44, 51, 54
    should be renounced, 58–59
Germany, use of bioweapons by, 12, 13
glanders, 13
Great Britain, 12, 92
Guterl, Fred, 35

Hamilton, Montana, 42–43
Harris, Elisa, 39
health care providers
  response to attacks by, 63–64, 68–69
  smallpox vaccination of, 78, 82
    opposition to, 74
    professional obligations and, 84–86, 87–88
hemorrhagic fevers, 43–44, 46
herd immunity, 87
Homeland Security Presidential Directive 10 (HSPD-10), 53
Horrock, Nicholas M., 40
hostage situations, 89–90
Hot Zone, The (Preston), 44
human physiology, manipulation of, 97–98

intelligence gathering, 65, 66–67
International Committee of the Red Cross, 97–98
Investigational New Drug (IND) protocols, 78–79
Iran, 39
Iraq, use of chemical weapons in, 28, 29, 94
Italy, 92–93

Japan, 13, 25, 29

Kampuchea (Cambodia), 12
Kaplan, Edward, 75
Kazakhstan, 35–36, 37–39

Kirker, Mary, 48
"knockout gas," 96
Kohenen, Anne, 17
Kurds, 28, 29

Laos, 12
law enforcement, chemical weapons
use by, 89–90, 91–93, 95, 96
Lawrence Livermore National
Laboratory, 42, 46
Leahy, Patrick, 7
Lebedev, Greg, 33
Lenihan, Patrick, 86
Lepyoshkin, Gennady, 37–38
Long Island, New York, 42
Los Alamos National Laboratory, 46

Mann, Susan, 46
Marburg disease, 43–44
May, Thomas, 81
McCarthy, Samantha, 46, 48
McLaughlin, Sabrina, 27
McVeigh, Timothy, 15
medicine stockpiles, 62, 76
Menino, Thomas, 49
Middle East, 18
"mirror-imaging," 52
moral disengagement techniques,
14–15
moral restraints, 14–15
Morocco, 92
Moscow (Russia), 89–90, 91
mustard gas, 28

National Biodefense Analysis and
Countermeasures Center (NBACC),
53–54, 68
National Bioforensic Analysis Center,
68
National Institutes of Health (NIH),
69
National Pharmaceutical Stockpile,
76
National Strategy to Combat Weapons
of Mass Destruction (report), 66
NBC news, 7
nerve gases, 7–8, 25
New York City, 7
New York Post (newspaper), 7
New York Times (newspaper), 55, 56

O'Toole, Tara, 13

Parker, Gerald W., 54
pathogens
availability of, 55–56
genetic engineering of, 44, 51, 54,
57, 58–59

Plum Island, 42
Preston, Richard, 44
Priesler, Steve, 13
Project BioShield, 62
Proliferation Security Initiative, 62,
66
public health officers
response to attacks by, 63–64,
68–69
smallpox vaccination and, 72
Public Health Security and
Bioterrorism Preparedness and
Response Act (2002), 45

al Qaeda, 36–37, 52
Q fever, 16

Red Teaming, 53
research
bioweapons
facilities for
opposition to location of,
41–43, 46–49
safety of, 42, 43–44, 45, 46–47,
55–56
secrecy about, 45
suspicions of other nations are
provoked by, 54–55
measures to build international
confidence and, 56–59
chemical weapons, 95–96, 97, 98
"dual-use," 58
funding for, 62–63
"Research Centers of Excellence," 47
Responsible Care Security Code
(American Chemistry Council),
32–34
Revolutionary War, 13
ricin, 52
Ridge, Tom, 32
ring vaccination, 75–76
riot control agents, 94–95
"rogue states," 37
Rumsfeld, Donald, 94
Russia
genetic engineering of anthrax in,
57
as partner in biodefense research,
57
smallpox repository in, 73
use of nonlethal chemical weapons
by terrorists in, 89–90, 91

sarin gas
attacks using, 25, 28, 29
effects of, 8
Scardaville, Michael, 71
Schelling, Thomas C., 11

Schumer, Charles, 42
Science-Based Threat Analysis and
    Response Program Office, 54
September 11, 2001 attacks, 11–12,
    15
Siegel, Marc, 22
Silent Death (Priesler), 13
Silverman, Ross D., 81
smallpox, 72–73
    U.S. vulnerability to attack with,
        24, 73–74
    vaccine stockpiles, 62
    voluntary vaccination program for
        liability and compensation
            concerns of, 78–79, 82–83, 86
        should be instituted, 72, 73,
            75–78, 79–80
        con, 73, 74, 82, 83–88
        standards for, 77
Smallpox Personnel Protection Act
    (2003), 83
Smithson, Amy, 30, 38
Somalia, 73
Soviet Union
    former
        bioweapons in, 35–36, 37–39
        weaponizing of smallpox in, 73
    genetic engineering of pathogens
        in, 51
    use of chemical and biological
        weapons by, 12, 13
    see also Russia
Spain, 92
Stepnogorsk weapons facility, 37–38
Stern, Jessica, 14–15
Stetson, Stephen, 8
Stevens, Robert, 7
Strategic National Stockpile of
    medicines, 62
Sun (newspaper), 7
Sunshine Project, 43
Synthetic Organic Chemical
    Manufacturers Association
    (SOCMA), 32

tabun gas, 8, 28
tear gas, 93–94
Tenet, George, 37
terrorists
    attacks on food supply by, 17–18,
        62, 64, 67
    bioweapons research facilities make
        communities targets for, 41, 48
    interest of, in chemical agents, 8
    lack moral restraints, 14–15
    protecting chemical plants from,
        30, 31–34
    pursuit of bioweapons by, 52

September 11, 2001 attacks by,
    11–12, 15
use of nonlethal chemical weapons
    by, 89–90, 91, 92
WMDs and, 36–37
Textbook for Military Medicine, 12
Tucker, Jonathan B., 50

UC Davis. *See* California, University
    of, at Davis
Ultimate Terrorists, The (Stern), 14–15
"Uncle Fester," 13
Union Carbide, 30
United States
    bioweapons facilities and scientists
        in former Soviet Union and,
        38–39
    bioweapons program of, 14
    compliance with CWC by, 96
    Defense Department
        biodefense role of, 65
        smallpox vaccination program of,
            74
    Environmental Protection Agency
        (EPA), 30
    Food and Drug Administration
        (FDA), 78–79
    Health and Human Services
        Department (HHS)
        biodefense role of, 44, 65–66, 69
        increase in research funding for,
            62
        smallpox vaccination program
            and, 75–76
    Homeland Security Department
        (DHS)
        biodefense role of, 64, 67, 68, 69
        chemical plants and, 33
        risk assessment of biological
            threats and, 53–54
    military
        budget of, 11
        possible attacks on, 18–20
        smallpox vaccination of
            personnel in, 72, 74
    national security of
        requires development of
            biodefense program, 21
        voluntary smallpox vaccination
            program would enhance, 72,
            79–80, 87
    State Department biodefense role,
        64–65
    use of nonlethal chemical weapons
        by, 93–94
Utah State University, 43

Vector Laboratories (Russia), 73

Vietnam War, 93
VX gas, 8, 25, 28

water supply safety, 64, 67
weapons of mass destruction
   (WMDs), 18–20, 36–37, 62
   see also bioweapons; chemical
   weapons
Wells, Miriam, 47–48
Wheelis, Mark, 89

Winder, Robert, 31
World Health Organization (WHO),
   73
World Trade Center
   1993 attack on, 14–15, 29–30
   2001 attack on, 11–12, 15
World War I, 12, 13, 92, 93
World War II, 13, 24–25

Yousef, Ramzi, 14–15